Contents

List of Illustrations

The Life and Music
of Brian Boydell

Editors

GARETH COX
AXEL KLEIN
MICHAEL TAYLOR

IRISH ACADEMIC PRESS
DUBLIN • PORTLAND, OR

First published in 2004 by
IRISH ACADEMIC PRESS
44 Northumberland Road, Dublin 4, Ireland

and in the United States of America by
IRISH ACADEMIC PRESS
c/o ISBS, Suite 300, 920 NE 58th Avenue
Portland, OR 97213-3786

Website: www.iap.ie

British Library Cataloguing in Publication Data

A catalogue record of this book is
available from the British Library.

ISBN 0-7165-2762-6

Library of Congress Cataloging-in-Publication Data

A catalog record of this book is
available from the Library of Congress.

Typeset in 11/13pt ClassGaramond by Irish Academic Press
Printed by Colourbooks, Dublin

Preface

Brian Boydell (1917–2000) is recognised as one of Ireland's leading twentieth-century composers with a rich and varied output stretching over fifty years. However, he also exerted an enormous influence on generations of musicians as Professor of Music at Trinity College Dublin, where he taught from 1962 to 1982, and as conductor of both the Dublin Orchestral Players for over twenty years and director of the Dowland Consort for some ten years. He was also a founder member of the Music Association of Ireland, a long-time member of the Arts Council and Aosdána, and recorded over 1,000 broadcasts. This book discusses the main characteristics of his compositional technique, considers his legacy as a historical musicologist researching eighteenth-century Dublin, and catalogues his works and writings. It also examines his fascinatingly rich life as musician, painter and general enthusiast.

The editors wish to acknowledge the kind cooperation of the Boydell family in the production of this book. They also wish to thank the Contemporary Music Centre, Ireland for permission to reproduce copyright material, Linda Longmore and Jonathan Manley of Irish Academic Press for their invaluable assistance, and Trinity College Dublin for a generous publication grant.

CHAPTER ONE

Brian Boydell: of man and music

AXEL KLEIN

Brian Patrick Boydell was born in Dublin on St Patrick's Day (17 March), 1917.[1] His family hailed originally from Leigh, Lancashire, and it was his grandfather who in the early 1870s made the move to Ireland. Both Boydell's grandfather and father were active in a profitable malting company which supplied malt mainly to Guinness and Jameson. Brian was also destined for a career in the family firm, and indeed after returning home from his studies in England and Germany, he worked for about a year as a biochemist in the company's laboratory before losing interest in the business.

From his early years, Boydell reacted strongly against imposed and outdated traditions. These reactions were first stimulated through his family, where he experienced conflicting views on the newly ruling Irish Catholic majority. Contrary to his father James Boydell, 'who believed that the King of England was appointed by God',[2] his mother, Eileen Collins, occasionally held nationalistic views considered unorthodox for one of her situation and background (she was, incidentally, one of the earliest women graduates of Trinity College, Dublin). The Protestant custom of sending one's children to school in England could also be problematic. He was first sent to Dragon School, Oxford, and afterwards to public school at Rugby. At Rugby he was asked 'not to make his nationality an excuse for his behaviour' and clearly felt 'that the system was geared towards inculcating empire-building values based on the arrogant assumption that God, through the Church of England, had given to the British establishment a superior knowledge of what was the right way for the rest of the world to behave'.[3] On the other hand, he found in his music teacher Kenneth Stubbs a person who became in many ways a father figure for him, perhaps compensating for his own rather strict father who displayed such little interest in music.[4] In his last year at Rugby he specialised in his two main fields of interest, music and the natural sciences.

Rugby also laid the foundations for his pacifist views and religious scepticism. He was thrown out of a compulsory military training corps and began to reject the use of force as a means towards political ends generally. His strong pacifist feelings led to the conclusion that no church anywhere in the world had dealt adequately with the question of violence.

At Rugby he had become an ardent Irish republican and admirer of de Valera, but a general distrust against nationalist ideologies developed after his return to Ireland. For here he found the same kind of attitude unwillingly directed against his own person when his attempts to be accepted as an Irishman failed because of his accent. He says, '… the Irish language was being used as a political entrance-ticket to such acceptance. I reacted in the opposite direction. The scales were by no means tipped completely: But I ended up with a distaste for all aspects of nationalist fervour and the emotional pressures of the propaganda that accompanies it.'[5]

Contributing to this attitude, of course, was the additional experience of another, more extreme, version of nationalism which he encountered in 1935 during his six-month stay in Heidelberg, Germany. Though this stay was primarily motivated by a wish to broaden his general education, learn the language and to hear as much first-class music as possible, in retrospect the violence experienced after, for instance, coming across a burned-out Jewish village, was extremely disturbing. In Heidelberg, Boydell received tuition at the Evangelisches Kirchenmusikalisches Institut with Meinhard Poppen (organ) and took private piano lessons with Friedrich Schery. He also travelled as far as Munich to a Wagner Festival and to see Richard Strauss conduct his *Die Frau ohne Schatten*.

Boydell had secured his place at Cambridge University before he went to Heidelberg: 'Life at Cambridge proved to be the fulfilment of dreams for one who wished to stretch his wings and discover what intellectual stimulus could be found through the freedom of uninhibited flight'.[6] He became a personal friend of Boris Ord, the organist and choirmaster at King's College and conductor of the University Madrigal Society. Edward Dent, the influential musicologist and first president of the International Society of Contemporary Music (ISCM), encouraged the college's 'Echo Club', a forum for the performance and the discussion of student compositions. Nevertheless, his first concern was the natural sciences tripos – geology, organic and biochemistry, physiology – a precondition of his father's to a later study of music.

Together with other musically interested students Boydell listened to 'cult works' on new gramophone recordings such as Alban Berg's *Lyric Suite*, and on 'carefully planned occasions we would listen to the newly available recordings with all lights extinguished. A period of meditation would follow during which no one would breathe a word that might disturb the magic spell.'[7]

Having successfully completed his studies at Cambridge with a First Class degree Boydell began studying composition at the Royal College of Music (RCM) in London in 1938. He enrolled with Patrick Hadley (1899–1973) and also, occasionally, when Hadley became the victim of his drinking problem, with Herbert Howells (1892–1983). Boydell remembered a lasting experience from this dual teaching in his autobiographical memories:

> I had just completed a song-setting, which I brought to Paddy. 'That's a very slimy-crawly bass,' he said; 'let's have some decent manly jumps and get rid of these chromatic intervals.' I took his advice and rewrote the song. Next week Paddy was on the booze, so I brought the song along to Herbert Howells. 'That's a very angular bass – especially for such a tender romantic poem! What about some sensuous chromatic intervals to create an emotional mood?' The complete contradiction between the opinion of two respected teaching composers puzzled me, until I came to realise that, apart from pure technique, effective creative expression can only be developed through rigorous self-criticism.[8]

In London, he also studied the oboe at the RCM (with William Henry Shepley), took piano lessons privately with a Solomon-pupil and lessons in voice production with Louise Trenton. At a student society for the performance of contemporary music Boydell sang songs by Schönberg, Berg and Bartók. Intense late-night discussions among fellow students were aroused by concerts at a Sibelius-festival under Thomas Beecham's direction. This period of study in London was cut short by the outbreak of war in 1939.

* * *

The forced return to a more peaceful Ireland meant that the musical experiences were limited compared to both Heidelberg and London. Boydell admits that he may have given an impression of arrogance with some Dublin musicians because he felt that his musical background was necessarily broader than that of most of his fellow-composers. Much later he came to regret some of his former reactions and conceded that this may have added to the non-acceptance he experienced after a while: 'I shudder when I think of some of the arrogant and tactless criticisms which I was guilty of levelling at Dublin musical life before developing a more mature relationship with people of varying views.'[9]

The full extent of these attitudes was not felt immediately as at first the circle of his friends comprised rather tolerant Anglo-Irish intellectuals and artists with an international outlook. Foremost among them was the 'White Stag' group of modern painters and sculptors. His membership in this gathering of modern artists was preceded by a teaching post at St Columba's College in south Dublin where he was asked to take over the art classes. Though, in his own assessment, a reasonable amateur painter, he wished to expand his own knowledge and techniques of painting and became a pupil of Mainie Jellett. For a while he pursued this part-time job in parallel with his work at the family malting company, but the more he became involved with Dublin artistic life and began earning an income by teaching art and by singing and playing the oboe, the more he was able to concentrate on artistic work.

In retrospect Boydell described his role with the White Stag group as a fringe membership because at around the same time (the early war years) he was becoming increasingly involved with music (in fact, there was no membership list or even a statement of the group's artistic aims). Nevertheless he participated in the annual Living Art Exhibitions in autumn with paintings he had done largely on the Aran Islands. However, the feeling that he would never quite achieve enough facility in draughtsmanship while his musical activities were at the same time expanding, led him to drop painting completely. 'Towards the end of 1944 I made the decision to devote my energies to music. Much as I may have been tempted I have never painted since.'[10]

After his RCM studies were interrupted by the outbreak of war, Boydell continued his musical studies with John F. Larchet (1884–1967), professor of harmony and counterpoint at the Royal

Irish Academy of Music (RIAM), during 1940 to 1942, when he gained an external Mus.B. from Trinity College.

The early war years were exciting ones for Brian Boydell in many respects. He tried his hand at many arts and trades before music eventually took over (almost) completely. It is less well-known, for instance, that he was, for a while, interested in puppet plays and in fact wrote a piece for the Dublin Marionette Group. A surrealist piece of his called *Revelation at Low Tide* was produced at the Peacock Theatre in November 1944 for which he also wrote incidental music and was a speaker at the performances. He commented on it: 'Most of the critics failed to find any meaning or sense in my play. I didn't intend that there should be any logic or sense in what was just a dreamlike surrealist evocation of a disturbing mood-picture.'[11]

The general petrol shortage during the war years was exploited by Boydell and his friends Grattan Norman and Lionel Kerwood to open a commercial company called Norman, Boydell & Kerwood Ltd. It specialised in equipping cars with an alternative driving system based on charcoal. This was burned in a large cylinder mounted at the back of a car, producing a mixture of carbon monoxide and unchanged nitrogen from the air, called producer gas. Using this rather susceptible but working system he was one of the very few in Ireland still able to drive a car by 1944 and even went on his honeymoon in June of that year with an old Sunbeam running on producer gas. Old and vintage cars were another field of interest and he used to possess a number of historic cars such as Bugattis and Sunbeams which he bought in run-down condition and repaired himself.

* * *

By this stage the acknowledged compositions of Brian Boydell consisted of a number of songs, his opus 1 being a setting of the poem 'Wild Geese' by P.H.B. Lyon (the headmaster at Rugby) for low voice and piano from 1935. His opus 2, Variations on 'The Snowy Breasted Pearl' (1936) for piano appears to be his only excursion into the area of folk-song adaptation. Song settings of poems by Joyce, Yeats and others followed. The largest early piece is the cantata *Hearing of Harvests* op. 13 (1940) for baritone, mixed voice chorus and orchestra, a 25-minute setting of a poem by W.H. Auden. The first work for symphony orchestra was the short tone poem *Laïsh*, op. 17 (1942), premiered by the Dublin Orchestral Players conducted by Havelock Nelson. He was to take over the baton of this amateur orchestra in the following year and became well known all over Ireland before he was forced to relinquish it in 1966 due to increasing teaching commitments.

However, the first step to recognition was inspired by the artistic community. As it was quite usual for a painter or sculptor to display his work in a one-man-show, Boydell adapted the practice for music by renting a room in the Shelbourne Hotel (with the help of his father) and presenting a collection of chamber music pieces. While orchestral music was becoming *en vogue* in Ireland at just about this time, the situation for ambitious chamber music was still quite different and probably the reason why Charles Acton later recalled this event as a 'protest'.[12] The pieces performed were the Three Songs, op. 10 (1939) for soprano and string quartet, the Quintet, op. 11 (1940) for oboe and string quartet, and first performances of the String Trio, op. 21 (1943) and *The Feather of Death*, op. 22 (1944) for baritone, flute, violin, viola, and violoncello. Boydell participated himself as baritone and oboist and his wife-to-be Mary sang in his opus 10. Charles Acton reported that this recital 'brought the begrudgers out alleging conceit, when he had to do it to put before the public that there was a composer there, in the days before Radio Éireann encouraged new Irish composition'. The fame of Brian Boydell as the 'bad boy' of Irish music had begun to spread.

The directorship of the Dublin Orchestral Players brought with it a welcome opportunity to have his own works studied and publicly performed – a most valuable experience and another factor which added to his reputation. Among his works performed were the *Satirical Suite*, op. 18a (1942) and the Symphony for Strings op. 26 (1945). Needless to say, many other Irish composers were performed, too, such as John Beckett, Edgar M. Deale or T.C. Kelly. The orchestra also presented many first Irish performances of standard classics or modern European classics. One of the more curious highlights was, according to Boydell,

> I believe ... the first and only performance in Ireland of the symphony by Beethoven which we don't mention, 'Wellington's Victory'. ... Beethoven, in this so-called 'Battle Symphony' asks in the score for French and English cannons, representing the opposing forces at the Battle of Vittoria. We wrote a letter to the *Evening Mail* requesting the loan of a pair of cannon for a forth-

coming symphony concert. This extraordinary unexplained request gave rise to banner headlines such as 'Musicians go to war!' and 'Mr Boydell in the bomber command'.

The second movement of the piece, which features variations on the British national anthem, was omitted, however, although the reaction of the audience had been eagerly anticipated.

To many Irish people the name of Brian Boydell was for many years connected with the educational programme of the Dublin Orchestral Players, the first orchestra to visit schools in Dublin and the provinces explaining the instruments of the orchestra. For many, this was the first contact with classical music in any form.

To others, he became known as a broadcaster, who from the mid-1940s began to present radio programmes in music appreciation – at first, it should perhaps be said, presented live from the studio with 78 rpm gramophone records and mostly without a written script. Altogether, Brian Boydell has presented some 1,000 programmes for Radio (Telefís) Éireann on many diverse subjects ranging from famil-iar international classics to Irish contemporary music.

In his autobiographical memoirs Boydell recounts that around this time the Head of the BBC Third Programme was in Dublin and he contacted him in a bar. After introducing himself, he

> asked whether the Third Programme would be interested in a talk about contemporary Irish composers, about whom little was known in England at the time. 'I'm sure that would be most inter-esting, Mr Boydell; but, you see, I was given strict instructions by our programme committee not to arrange for anything of a purely parochial nature.' Now I am quite sure that every one of us has been faced with the situation where it would be wonder-ful to be quick-witted enough to produce just the right reply on occasions such as this … Only twice in my life do I remember having the good fortune to think of the right remark to counter such a patronising insult – and on this occasion, it just happened to fall out of my mouth when I replied: 'But you do have talks about English composers, don't you?' Needless to say; I was not asked to sign a contract.[13]

Following his appointment as Professor of Singing at the RIAM in 1944 and with more engagements as oboist, singer, broadcaster and composer of incidental music at the Olympia Theatre, Brian Boydell was able more and more to make a living from his music. His period of teaching at the RIAM (until 1952) coincided happily with a time in which he wrote some of the compositions he will be most remembered by: the orchestral pieces *Symphony for Strings*, op. 26 (1945), the Five Joyce Songs, op. 28 (1946), *In Memoriam Mahatma Gandhi*, op. 30 (1948), the String Quartet No. 1, op. 31 (1949) and the cantata *Timor Mortis*, op. 35 (1952), which was later incorporated into the work *Mors et vita*, op. 50 (1961). His Violin Concerto, op. 36 of 1953 was written just after that time and revised one year later.

* * *

The founding of the Music Association of Ireland (MAI) in 1948 was due to the efforts of Brian Boydell, Frederick May, Edgar M. Deale and the music critic Michael McMullin. It was felt that the existing musical societies were very much following their own individual aims and that some unification would be helpful for all sides. Many friends agreed to become sponsors and at a meeting on 13 April 1948 the Association was inaugurated.

From the perspective of the history of Irish composition the first meetings of composers within the MAI are even more interesting than the other aims and activities of the Association, which is still very active today. Apparently the first such meeting, on 30 October 1949, was not very well attended, but afterwards a 'large number of enthusiastic letters [were] received from those who were unable to attend'.[14] What developed into the 'Composers' Group' of the MAI, a forum for the discussion of scores and recordings of fellow members, had, in the beginning, clearly higher aims. Many reactions to a letter calling for a second, more representative meeting indicate that national representation was sought by many composers, and that this should develop into something like an Irish branch of the ISCM.[115]

The letter, signed by Brian Boydell, mentions the names of forty-one composers as addressees and each was asked to invite other composers he/she knew. It is an interesting list, ranging from names still known today (Brian Boydell, Frederick May, John F. Larchet, Aloys Fleischmann, Gerard Victory) to musicians with a smaller output (Arthur Duff, Walter Beckett, Edgar M. Deale, Brendan Dunne, George Hewson, Joseph Groocock), a list of female composers (Ina Boyle, Dorothy Parke, Rhoda Coghill, Kitty O'Callaghan and a 'Miss Pigott'), the more conservative musicians (Michael Bowles, Havelock Nelson, Daniel McNulty, Fachtna

Ó hAnnracháin, Thomas C. Kelly, Redmond Friel, Eamonn Ó Gallchobhaír), some immigrants (Ernest de Regge, Joseph Cuypers, Michael van Dessel, Staf Gebruers) and some names virtually forgotten today in the Irish world of composition such as Kevin Connolly, Jack Horn, Peter Killian, Philip Model, Patrick O'Malley, Thomas Weaving and others. Also listed is Geoffrey Molyneux Palmer (1882–1957), who in the 1980s achieved some fame for his neglected Joyce-songs, as well as Charles Lynch, the pianist, and Éimear O'Broin, the conductor, who also seems to have composed occasionally.

The letter is followed by two pages of quotations from some of the composers mentioned, outlining the aims a representative body should pursue. It was Ina Boyle (1889–1967) who here made the suggestion that a catalogue of Irish music should be published giving short particulars of works for international information – an idea finally realised in 1968 with a book edited by Edgar Deale for the MAI.[16] Aloys Fleischmann was 'very glad that we are considering breaking our disastrous isolation in music', and Geoffrey M. Palmer believed that 'affiliation to the ISCM could not be but beneficial'. Affixed to the document is a most interesting confidential list of names with signs indicating who is understood to write in a 'reasonably contemporary idiom' and who has 'very little original work as far as is known'.

This brief look at the background to the founding of the MAI shows clearly that Brian Boydell was instrumental in bringing this important organisation into life and in providing salient ideas. Many of the aims of the organisation such as a National Concert Hall and bringing music to the schools and to country areas are now a regular feature of Irish musical life. Boydell was correct when he surmised in his autobiography that the fact 'that so much musical effort is now promoted by professional administrators and supported by semi-state funding must owe something to our efforts of forty years ago'.[17]

* * *

The year 1948 also saw the expansion of the Irish radio orchestra into the Radio Éireann Symphony Orchestra – a date which is often misinterpreted as its founding.[18] The recruitment of the extra musicians was made largely on the European continent – many came from Eastern and Southern Europe, some from Germany or the Low

Countries – regions largely suffering the aftermath of the war at this time. These musicians were to lead their respective sections in the orchestra and were expected to take up teaching as well. From today's perspective, this period of creative influx represented a very valuable contribution to the development of music in Ireland.

What made this period so important for Brian Boydell was that it suited his predeliction for international contacts. In fact, in the course of the following years a number of friendships resulted from this creative mix of cultures. One example is the cellist Wolfram Hentschel who, together with François d'Albert, founded the Dublin String Quartet. On his return to Hamburg some years later he became a member of the Benthien String Quartet, which recorded Boydell's String Quartet No. 1 for the Deutsche Grammophon record company. In 1957, Boydell wrote his second string quartet for them. A lasting friendship evolved with the flautist André Prieur, founder of the Prieur Ensemble – for which Boydell wrote his Quintet op. 49 (1960) – and in 1970 of the New Irish Chamber Orchestra, the predecessor of today's Irish Chamber Orchestra. For the Italian clarinet player Michele Incenzo, Boydell wrote his *Elegy and Capriccio*, op. 42 for clarinet and strings (1956), performed with the Dublin String Orchestra conducted by the German Hermann Pöche. Boydell wrote in his autobiography: 'During the rehearsals, Michele was particularly delighted with the Capriccio, which has quite a showy part for the soloist. Every now and then, when Pöche was sorting out some detail in the string parts, he would run over to me, shake my hand violently, and declare in his wonderful Italianate English 'Very nice-a modern musica. I do-a my best-a!' He did. He played it brillantly!'[19]

There were also fond memories of the German choral conductor Hans Waldemar Rosen, conductor of the Radio Éireann (later RTÉ) Singers, and of the violinist Jaroslav Vanacek from Czechoslovakia, an influential teacher at the Municipal School of Music (later the College of Music, now the DIT Conservatory of Music and Drama). After a period of changing conductors, a new permanent conductor for the RÉSO was appointed in 1953, Milan Horvat from Zagreb. This partnership resulted in, among other things, the first recordings of orchestral music by contemporary Irish composers. The two volumes of 'New Music from Old Erin' for the American subsidiary of the Decca record company were obviously aimed at the American-Irish market to judge by the title and the cover, which depicted an old thatched cottage in rural Connemara. Volume 1 opened with Brian Boydell's *Megalithic Ritual Dances*, op. 39 (1956), his latest composition.[20]

The record was produced by Simon Rady, an American with a rather brash appearance and with 'pockets bursting with dollar bills', which, as Boydell recalls, obviously whetted the appetite of the orchestral musicians. Rady, however, also seems to have been an expert in acoustics and was equipped with an outstanding musical ear. Boydell remembers:

> ... the orchestra had been engaged for the first opportunity they were to enjoy of earning extra money outside their routine contract. They assembled for the first session in high spirits, rubbing their hands in glee at the promised share of dollars from the American they took to be an ignorant charlatan. Precisely at ten o'clock they started tuning up. The burly figure of Rady appeared on the balcony above the stage. In a tone of utterly dismissive sarcasm he drawled 'Do you call that an A? Clarinet, you're flat!' Michele Incenzo stood up waving his arms in excitable gestures of outrage and replied: 'I have-a a certificate from my professore in Napoli: my clarinetto plays a perfect 440 A!'
> 'I don't care how many bloody certificates you have; all the wind can go home, and don't dare come back here until you can play a proper A'. The wind skulked out with the tails between their legs and came back a chastened lot for the afternoon session. The recording proceeded with strings alone for the works that did not call for wind instruments.[21]

Boydell recalls that Simon Rady had at least as much influence on the recording as the conductor Milan Horvat. One example during the recording of his *Megalithic Ritual Dances* involved the third percussion player that the score called for. There were only two in the orchestra – the third would have had to play a 'tricky' tambourine part. It was Rady's decision not to ask a player from the Army Band which would have been the usual procedure – but to add this part to the tape some weeks later in Berlin with the first percussion player of the Berlin Philharmonic.

* * *

It was the critic Denis Donoghue who linked Boydell's professorship at the Royal Irish Academy of Music with Milan Horvat. He was a singing pupil of Boydell's at the RIAM and one of several with whom he formed a long-lasting friendship. When Horvat became principal conductor in 1953, Donoghue was music critic of the *Irish Times*. When a concert of Horvat's in 1955 received a most uncomplimentary review by Donoghue, it eventually led to the critic's resignation. The trouble was caused by none other than the later President of Ireland, Erskine Childers, then Minister for Posts and Telegraphs with responsibility for broadcasting – and therefore also for the orchestra and for the appointment of Horvat. In the face of the continuing criticism of Horvat since his appointment, Childers seems to have lost his good temper and sent for the paper's editor who in turn demanded that Donoghue tone down his criticism of Horvat. Donoghue replied that he would rather resign than sacrifice his integrity. Charles Acton, another good friend of Boydell's from his schooldays in England, became his successor.

In 1955, Denis Donoghue, who later became a respected professor of literature at New York University, wrote an important paper on the state of music in Ireland entitled 'The Future of Irish Music', published in the Jesuit periodical *Studies*. It has become an often quoted article in Irish musicology for it contains some provocative remarks such as 'there is in Ireland to-day no composer whose works an intelligent European musician must know'.[22] This appeared to shatter all the hopes that had emerged from developments of recent years such as the new generation of composers and the expansion of radio and concert audiences. Comparing 1955 with a list of performances of Irish music between 1935 and 1951 in Aloys Fleischmann's book *Music in Ireland* (Cork, 1952), Donoghue states that, of the twenty-nine composers mentioned in that book, not more than six would be capable of creative work today. Together with new names which sprang up since then the number might rise to nine or ten. Yet he says, 'internationally, Irish music does not exist' – a conclusion derived from the under-representation of Ireland at international festivals and on concert circuits (which, in turn, was partly due to the lack of an ISCM membership).

The only hope he saw on the Irish music horizon was Brian Boydell. 'Within the past few years it has become clear that Brian Boydell is the most active composer in Ireland: in my opinion he is also the best. I believe that if Irish music is to have any future he will form an important part of it, or rather, that if it is to develop at all it will do so on lines that he represents.'[23] This assessment was not influenced by his personal friendship, but rather from the fact that the majority of Irish composers still fell into 'the trap of folk-music',[24] whereas Boydell represented the cosmopolitan, middle-European side of modern classical music and as such was working practically alone in Ireland. To add a postscript to the Donoghue article, it should be noted, however, that its author – despite his many important and necessary observations – does not seem to have been aware of all the music which was written in Ireland at the time. Important pieces and new aspects of composers' *oeuvres* have only much later been discovered. Donoghue's article nevertheless stands out as a courageous and perceptive analysis and may be seen as representative of a view held by many when it comes to assessing Brian Boydell's importance at this time.

* * *

The status of music in Ireland around 1950 was a topic of much concern for composers, musicians and critics alike. In contemporary interdisciplinary journals, Aloys Fleischmann had engaged in the topic since the mid-1930s; Frederick May's papers in *The Bell* of 1947 and 1954 are outstanding examples; Charles Acton contributed a paper 'Towards an Irish Music' for *Envoy* in 1950 – and Brian Boydell himself added papers to the discussion, which were also important contributions to contemporaneous cultural discourse.

An interesting facet of Boydell's article 'Music in Ireland' in the April 1947 issue of *The Bell* is that most of the suggestions made therein to remedy the derelict situation of Irish music were later realised. His first point demonstrating the 'gloomy lines in this sad picture of the state of musical endeavour in Ireland to-day'[25] was the fact that no orchestral concerts had yet been heard outside the capital (the MAI, founded one year later, were the first to rectify this). The criticism that the national orchestra was too small was responded to one year later with the influx of foreign musicians described above. Boydell's now famous remark that the orchestra was all too often forced to perform 'in the form of meal-time concerts for those who prefer to eat their sausages and mash to the background of trivial light music',[26] was also responded to soon after by the foundation of the Radio Éireann Light Orchestra – today the RTÉ Concert Orchestra. Chamber music, he writes, was almost entirely neglected by Irish musicians – but as was outlined above, this state of affairs changed with the many musicians from Italy, Hungary, France and Germany who founded chamber ensembles.

What, arguably, has not changed much is the tendency among Irish musicians to split into rival factions: in the 1940s Boydell regrets the existence of three opera companies, a dozen amateur orchestras and several schools of music in Dublin alone, which in his view impeded the growth of effective musical ensembles. The standard of musical criticism was also a source of much debate (and has been ever since) – today one notes the pitifully small amount of space devoted to classical music in the press generally. Boydell's most serious point, the inadequate situation of music education in the sense of a developed general appreciation of music as art remains a deplorable aspect of Irish culture.

'Culture and Chauvinism', published in *Envoy* in 1950, represents Boydell's plea for a more cosmopolitan orientation for Irish culture. 'It may be very pleasant to lock oneself in the bathroom away from the dangerous influence of the rabble outside, and listen to the sweet reverberations of one's own voice; but it is not a very constructive occupation, and is inclined to give one an undue opinion of one's own vocal powers'[27] – a more succinct comment on contemporary developments in Irish culture is hard to find. What follows is a positive interpretation of nationalism in music arguing that Irish composers should allow for natural expressions of their creativity, which will inevitably produce a discernible Irish music without overemphasising one's nationhood. 'Any artist who is Irish, and is sensitive to the strong and individual atmosphere of his country cannot help expressing the Irish spirit in his work; and it is his peculiar viewpoint which is a contribution to the Art of the World.'[28] This is a trenchant summary of much of Boydell's creative output, and its consequences can be found not only in the much-quoted Violin Concerto (1953–54), but in fact in quite a number of his compositions.[29] Yet it is also a convincing clue to the fact that his music ranks, at the same time, among the most cosmopolitan music in Ireland of his time.

Four years before Denis Donoghue, Boydell published a similar article, 'The Future of Music in Ireland'.[30] He is no less provocative when he states 'that music in Ireland, in spite of superficial appearances, is in a shocking state'.[31] As always in his articles, Boydell does not confine himself to mere criticism but gives constructive suggestions as to how things might be improved. He sees four reasons for the present dismal situation. One is the tendency to 'do a great deal of talking in this country ... but positive action seldom follows all the talk'.[32] The second is the national characteristic of thinking in terms of the past, thus precluding pragmatic concepts for the future. Further, those in control of the money lack a sense for music as an artform which will 'never pay for itself on the materialistic level'.[33] Finally, the small size of the country appears to hinder the development of a large following for classical music; however, Boydell recommends looking at the positive example of Finland and considering such solutions as developing education, broadcasting, publishing, a concert hall and a national orchestra.

* * *

By the mid-1950s the musical scene in Ireland with regard to composition had begun to change. With Frederick May ceasing creative work, Aloys Fleischmann, A.J. Potter (1918–80) and Brian Boydell, for a short while, seemed to be the only 'serious' composers active. Then a new generation emerged with the first professional works by Gerard Victory (1921–95), Seán Ó Riada (1931–71) and Seóirse Bodley (b. 1933), and they were joined in the early 1960s by James Wilson (b. 1922) and John Kinsella (b. 1934). 'A Music Makers Portrait Gallery', published in the *Irish Times* on 2 July 1960, examines the question as to who at this time could fulfil the old Irish hope of providing the 'great national composer'. The author of the illustrated article is not named, but it is most likely that Charles Acton, the paper's music critic, wrote it. The chances for an important national role in music are ruled out completely for the 'folky composers' Walter Beckett, T.C. Kelly, Raymond [*sic*] Friel and Eamonn Ó Gallchobhair,[34] though in a traditional sense, their work would have been the most national. Not considered also are Havelock Nelson (1917–96) for his many activities outside the field of composition, and Gerard Victory for his 'slow development' – both merely receive a mention.

Among the remaining composers, Brian Boydell is the first to receive critical commentary. This is the first time that his potential is in doubt. Although the section on him begins: 'Foremost among the pure internationalists is Brian Boydell, whom we can regard as the leader of the middle aged composers', the author continues: 'As a busy lecturer, adjudicator, conductor and committee man, Dr Boydell seems to be developing very slowly as a composer … The next two years will decide whether Dr Boydell's talents are creative or didactic.'[35]

Acton in 1960 could not have foreseen that by 1962 Boydell would be professor of music at Trinity College. His personal relations with Boydell himself had cooled over the years and he wrote of him, as seen above, with a certain amount of professional detachment. However, Boydell knew by the end of the 1950s that George H.P. Hewson's professorship at TCD would soon come to an end. A number of people on the inside were encouraging Boydell to succeed him, as he related to Michael Dungan.[36] One requirement, however, was a doctoral degree, which he duly passed in 1959. 'In order to qualify myself for that I did the horrifying thing – having already become a reasonably established musician – of sitting an exam, terrified that I might fail. So I took the Doctorate of Music and luckily passed it.' Acton's speculation in 1960 that he might have a 'didactic' future proved correct, at least in a sense.

However, Acton never spared critical remarks about Boydell's music. In the 1960 *Irish Times* survey he writes that, with the exception of his first string quartet and the cantata *Timor Mortis*, op. 35 (1952),[37] 'all his work so far has technical and formal patches of tentativeness that detract from the total success and rob such deeply felt works as *La* [*sic*] *Memoriam Mahatma Gandhi* and the *Megalithic Ritual Dances* of their full effect'. Ten years later, at the end of his interview with Boydell published in *Éire-Ireland*, he explains that 'a decade or so ago he seemed to be in danger of solidifying into a musical personality of the 1930s. But I have the impression that in the last few years the inspiration of this pack of young students has melted the ice and started a new flow of adventurousness.'[38] One of the most convincing examples he saw was in Boydell's *Symphonic Inscapes*, op. 64 (1968) first performed on 26 January 1969 by the RTÉ Symphony Orchestra under Albert Rosen. In his review in the *Irish Times* Acton wrote that

> a major event was the first performance of Brian Boydell's new work ... To my mind this is, beyond doubt, the most accomplished orchestral work Dr Boydell has yet written, and I hope it may lead to a really fruitful advance. In all three movements, but especially in the first, he has solved with complete success his perennial problem of sustaining our interest. Too often, up to now, a climatic or important passage would suddenly lose all its tension and sag, with the result that our interest sagged too. Here, every thought leads on to the next, however much contrasted in mood or content.[39]

With this view Acton indicates that the professorship at Trinity College had the effect of a fountain of youth on Boydell's creativity. This was certainly of mutual benefit, because the college greatly profited from Boydell's tenure of office, which was to last until 1982. Since its inauguration in the eighteenth century the professorship at TCD had been a mere examining body – there was no academic study, and although in his last years his predecessor George Hewson had given some lectures, music had not been an academic course as such. Backed by the provost, Boydell completely modified the requirements of the degrees and liberated it from the dust of the nineteenth century. Looking at his own doctoral exam he later commented: 'It was rather like a senior Bachelor of Music: instead of doing four-part harmony you did six-part harmony and it was an entirely dull, academic thing. A most uninspiring exam. So I redesigned it and made it much more realistic as far as music is concerned.'[40]

Guided by such a pragmatic approach, one of his innovations for the bachelor's degree course was that the Renaissance compositional style was studied by first singing the music before analysing it. He established a full honours course in music requiring practical skills on an instrument but also catering for musicology. Studying music with Boydell made Trinity College an attractive place for aspiring composers, musicologists and musicians. Charles Acton wrote in 1970:

> In the few years that he has been Professor of Music of Dublin University, he has brought the Music Department to pulsating, vigorous life, helped, as he was, first, by a number of enthusiastic English student musicians and, in the last two or three years, by the presence in Dublin of a pack of music students across the frontiers of the schools and colleges across the musical disciplines who are being a real inspiration to practically every field of music in the capital at present.[41]

Some of his better known students were composers Eric Sweeney, Kevin O'Connell and Fergus Johnston, musicians such as harpsichordist Malcolm Proud, the organists Peter Sweeney and David Adams and violinist Maighread McCrann and musicologist Gareth Cox, to name but a few.

* * *

As Professor of Music at Trinity College from 1962 to 1982 and as the longest-serving member of the Arts Council from 1961 to 1983, Brian Boydell steered a good deal of the development of music in Ireland during these years. His influence on cultural politics is difficult to assess. He admits that in the early years democracy in the Arts Council's decisions was not always easy to achieve. In Brian Kennedy's account of Irish cultural politics between the founding of the Free State and the late 1980s Boydell is quoted as saying:

> I had the impression that everything was fixed beforehand by Fr. O'Sullivan.[42] Things ran on the nod without any hitches. Michael Scott was in collusion with Fr. O'Sullivan and they decided things together. There was an awkward quality about having a priest as Director. Firstly, at that time among Catholics there was a tremendous respect for priests and you never criticised them or disagreed with their opinion. Secondly, anyone like me reared in an Anglo-Irish Protestant background could never criticise a priest or it would invite a clamour of protest about being anti-Catholic and having no respect.[43]

On the other hand, for the entire decade of the 1960s Boydell was the only creative artist on the council sitting alongside administrators and politicians. As such he lobbied hard for artists' needs, however it may often have seemed futile.

Less of a struggle was another 'public service' for music – Boydell's 'affair' with the national anthem. Commissioned by Radio Éireann in 1961 for the beginning of the Irish television age, it was to be the piece played at the end of the TV broadcast each night, and accompanied with pictures of the Irish countryside and other national symbols. Boydell's arrangement was chosen after a competition among Irish composers and after having consulted a Mr Byrne, a Canadian Consultant for Radio Éireann, for advice on how best to proceed. Byrne told Boydell: 'I wan' it BIG! I envisage the kind of music that will stir the hearts of the Irish people. Now I don't know a great deal about music, but I'm thinking of great rolls on the drums, stirring fanfares of trumpets and a really BIG sound – to accompany a film shot of the tanks and men of the Irish army proceeding down O'Connell Street in a grand procession.'[44]

As president of the Irish Pacifist Movement and a convinced member of Amnesty International such words almost made Boydell decline the commission. But he regarded it more as a challenge, a challenge to clothe a simple and undistinguished tune (The Soldiers'

Song) in a new garment 'that would raise its musical value and lend it some sense of dignity'. He continues:

> ... with a certain element of cynicism remaining (as I remembered the advice to 'make it BIG') I chose the largest sheet of manuscript paper that I could find, saying to myself 'I'll fill every line of that immense orchestral score if I can possibly manage it'. Harp, organ, off-stage trumpets and a battery of percussion (for the 'great roll on the drums') accounted for a large number of those lines ... I completed the score on 6 July 1961 and awaited judgement. To my surprise my arrangement was chosen.[45]

So beginning on 31 December 1961, RTÉ ended its programme for many decades with Boydell's arrangement of the National Anthem. Had he not been paid by contract for the copyright of the complete arrangement, he might have made a small fortune just by the rights to play the first three bars, which consist of original music which Boydell composed himself.

* * *

Brian Boydell continued his close association with Radio (Telefís) Éireann and its orchestra well into the 1960s. With the arrival in 1962 of Tibor Paul, the Hungarian-born naturalised Australian who succeeded Milan Horvat as conductor of the orchestra, Boydell's role became even more involved. As Paul's personality tended to be confrontational, many musicians were unwilling to continue under his leadership (in fact, the Ulster Orchestra in Belfast, founded in 1966, was largely made up of 'refugees' from Dublin as a result).

He described his new role and its background thus:

> [Tibor Paul] was a very clever operator, soon edging his way into being appointed Director of Radio Music in addition to his being chief conductor. The result was that members of the orchestra had no one to whom they could appeal if they felt that they were being unjustly treated by the conductor. Kevin McCourt, the Director of Broadcasting, who had the final say, found himself out of his depth; for he was inexperienced in dealing with musicians. This is where I came in; for Kevin, knowing that I had no particular axe to grind and was on friendly terms with both parties, invited me to act as his confidential music adviser.[46]

One of the occasions when Boydell had to step in was when Paul –

more or less with his own career in mind – planned a tour of the United States, the cost of which would have surpassed the orchestra's annual budget. The tour had to be cancelled, but Paul apparently manipulated his close contacts with the press and managed to embarrass McCourt with headlines such as 'Director of Broadcasting Cancels Great Opportunity for Irish Orchestra in America'. With Boydell's diplomatic talents the matter was smoothed over for the musicians and the public.

Tibor Paul nevertheless appears to have been an accomplished orchestral trainer and an influential personality. One of his memorable achievements was to persuade Igor Stravinsky to visit Dublin and conduct a number of his works in 1963.[47] From reading various descriptions of Stravinsky's scathing remarks about other composers, Boydell had the impression that the great composer would not be a very pleasant man to meet. Yet Tibor Paul insisted on introducing the two. Boydell says:

> He was absolutely charming. If only I could have made a tape recording to accompany the photograph I have of that meeting! I was just introduced as an Irish composer. My name obviously meant nothing to him, but lest he put his foot in it he played safe. Beaming at me he greeted me with 'Ah … Brian Boydell! I have heard your music with great pleasure in New York, in Tokyo and in Paris. It is a great honour to meet you in person!'
>
> It was only when Arthur Nachstern, a Polish immigrant violinist, was introduced to him that the veneer of charm cracked and showed the vituperative side to his character. Arthur spoke of the great pleasure he had enjoyed playing the Firebird Suite under Ernest Ansermet, who was credited with playing an important part in Stravinsky's early successes. The benign smile was replaced with a frowning scowl. 'Ansermet … he was a bad man! He ruined so many performances of my music.'[48]

* * *

Despite the professorship and his other commitments, Boydell for a while continued to adjudicate at music competitions all over Ireland, Britain and as far afield as Canada. He was also active as a guest conductor (e.g. with the CBC Symphony Orchestra) and he made a name for himself conducting a semi-professional vocal ensemble, the Dowland Consort, which he founded and directed since 1958. This ensemble corresponded with his long-time love for Renaissance vocal music, a love he cherished since his student days at Cambridge. There he had been on a choral scholarship, and was also a member of the Cambridge Madrigal Society of Clare College under the direction of Boris Ord.

During the 1960s the Dowland Consort established itself firmly on the Irish musical map. In his unpublished autobiography Boydell explains the secret of the ensemble's quick success:

> In those days music from four hundred years ago was considered much more 'highbrow' and reserved for academic study than it is now. In order to break down these barriers and draw in a wider public, we planned an approach to concert-giving which was aimed at informal communication. Instead of standing stiffly in well-ordered ranks we attempted to create the relaxed and intimate atmosphere of domestic music making by sitting informally around a semi-circular table ... I sat at one end, directing the ensemble, and I introduced each item, providing translations for the pieces in Italian, French or German.[49]

The second baritone alongside Boydell was Tomás Ó Súilleabháin (one of the most important champions of contemporary Irish music at the time), Cáit and Dick Cooper sang soprano and tenor respectively while the other three sopranos were Mary Boydell, Eilís O'Sullivan and Gráinne Yeats. Altos were Hazel Morris and Enid Chaloner, while the second tenor was Leonard Jose, who was later replaced by George Bannister.

The first public appearance of the Dowland Consort was on 10 April 1959 in Dublin and they received enthusiastic public and critical responses. They performed in all major Irish towns, as well as in London's Wigmore Hall, Chester, Liverpool and Manchester. They broadcast recitals for RTÉ (fourteen times) and the BBC (ten times) and were presented with the Harriet Cohen International Music Award in 1964. They also published an LP recording during this time for the Alpha label (AVM 021, 'Renaissance Lieder and Chansons'), which included a number of pieces in English, French and German.

During the eleven years of the Consort's existence, the ensemble had a repertoire of more than 300 works – Boydell's own records show that they amounted to 96 English madrigals, 90 Italian madrigals, villanelles, etc., 43 French chansons and 32 German lieder in addition to 15 complete masses and 31 religious motets by altogether more than 70 different composers. The most frequently performed composer was Monteverdi, and it is largely through this promotion of early Italian culture in Ireland that Boydell was awarded the honorary title of Commendatore de la Repubblica Italiana in 1983. The ensemble disbanded in 1969. Boydell recalls that

> perhaps the most gratifying outcome of the career of the Dowland Consort was not a purely musical one: though it does, I think, demonstrate the benign power of music. When we came together ... we were a very heterogeneous bunch of individuals as far as background is concerned. Irish-speaking nationalists, Protestant Anglo-Irish, married and un-married, and whatever other cultural differences you can think of. Our experience of working together in the performance of music had the effect of welding the members of the consort into a family of life-long friends. We still meet together two or three times a year, enjoy a good meal, and follow it by singing favourite pieces from our repertoire (perhaps I should say that we now croak our way through them!).[50]

* * *

'I'm terribly aware that I am now an old fogey', Boydell said in 1992,[51] repeating a description of himself from as early as 1970,[52] and alluding to his conscious choice of eschewing certain modern compositional trends. 'That means that I am not interested in writing what I call ping-pong music – you know, the sort of thing that goes ping once and pong another time with some curious noise in the middle.' Boydell's arguments as to his belief in tonality were always explicit as they supported his own admission of being an 'old fogey'. The image will have been a fitting one for many of the young students of the Trinity professor and the audience and participants in the 1970s Dublin Festivals of Twentieth-Century Music. For most of these, Irish composition had only just begun and many of this new generation of composers born around or after the mid-1940s believed that they worked in an historical vacuum, that Irish art music had no tradition in the country. For them, Brian Boydell's musical voice was conservative and it was hard to believe that he was once the 'naughty boy' of Irish music in the distant 1940s.

However, history's perspective has changed unrecognisably and whole generations of twentieth-century composers who suffered neglect in the 1960s and 1970s craze for serial or minimalist music are now being rediscovered. As twentieth-century music history can not be regarded anymore as a single direct line unerringly proceeding from Schoenberg via Berg, Webern, Nono, Stockhausen and Boulez to Ferneyhough and Lachenmann, the musical achievement of Brian Boydell must attract musicological and analytical attention. The next chapter, by Gareth Cox, presents a detailed analysis of his musical language.

Since Harry White deals with Boydell as musicologist, suffice to say that with his (re-)discovery and exploration of Irish musical history in the eighteenth century, Brian Boydell not only found another outlet for his talents; he also demonstrated that twentieth-century Irish music did not develop from a *tabula rasa*, that Ireland indeed has a classical music history which is worth studying, reviving and recording.

* * *

A biographical sketch such as this obviously does not replace a full and comprehensive biography which would discuss the human dimensions of many personal events in Brian Boydell's life such as the tragedy that befell the Boydells when they lost their youngest son Marnac (b. 1955) in a motorbike accident in 1981. It might also explore more about his own family and the fact that his wife is a glass expert, that his eldest son Cormac (b. 1946) is a much respected artist living and working on the Beara Pensinsula, or that Barra (b. 1947) is one of Ireland's leading musicologists at the National University of Ireland at Maynooth. Brian Boydell's life story is so rich and so multifaceted that he stands out as one of the most fascinating and remarkable Irishmen of the twentieth century.

CHAPTER TWO

The musical language of Brian Boydell: octatonic and diatonic interaction

GARETH COX

Boydell's musical language throughout his compositional career was marked by his consistent and original use of the octatonic scale and its subsets, most particularly in interaction with diatonic collections. I briefly explored this aspect of Boydell's language in an article in *Irish Musical Studies* in 1996 where I concluded that, 'however free this employment and integration of octatonicism is, it is clear that it has provided him with compositional material which has resulted in a style that is eminently comprehensible and coherent'.[1] In addition, it has not only secured his position as one of the most important and individual Irish composers of the twentieth century, but it also places him in an international context with other composers whose music displays significant octatonic elements such as *inter alia*, Stravinsky, Bartók, and Messiaen.

He often described the development of his compositional style as a reaction to 'the Stanford-Harty Anglo-Irish tradition'.[2] His influences were eclectic and he has stated that 'the European influences which affected our music in the early Forties included a shared admiration of Berg, Vaughan Williams, Sibelius and Mahler [and that] Moeran and Bax ... also had an influence, and Delius was hovering somewhere in the background'.[3] In fact he appears to have been influenced by most of the major composers from the first half of the twentieth century with the exception of Schoenberg and Webern, having made a clear decision not to venture down the serialist path. In an interview with Hazel Farrell, he repeated his oft-stated aversion to serialism and suggested that he was influenced, if by any composer, 'by the theories, rather than the actual music, of Hindemith'.[4] In a seminar in Belfast in 1969 he had also been 'at pains to stress his reaction against those present-day composers who were determined to compose within particular systems'.[5] He mentions Bartók as the 'abiding' influence and also felt that he 'must have been influenced by Prokofiev' as well.[6] He described his work as being very intuitive and believed totally in 'communication as the fundamental motive'.[7] He reiterated this in an interview in 1997 by insisting that 'I write music that I like'[8] and that he has 'always tried to create sounds which [he] honestly believe[s] to be expressive or beautiful'.[9] It all boils down to his own statement that his musical language emanates from 'a firm belief in artistic honesty: creating sounds that I like personally'.[10]

Boydell was a craftsman with a complete mastery of functional tonality and well-schooled in traditional forms and neo-classical techniques. He also had a command of orchestration the equal of his contemporary A.J. Potter (1918–80). Rhythmically he was probably most influenced by Bartók. The hallmark of his style, however, is manifestly revealed in a study of the juxtaposition of diatonicism (both implied and overt) and octatonicism, evident in most of his major works. I wish now to trace this octatonic/diatonic interaction and Boydell's use of octatonic sets and subsets as displayed in thematic and motivic material in selected works by drawing on the methodology of Pieter van den Toorn and Allen Forte.[11]

His use of the octatonic scale of alternating tones and semitones and its subsets since the end of the 1940s was noted by Boydell himself although he was quick to point out that it came uncon-sciously during the creative process.[12] Indeed the term octatonic was not coined by Arthur Berger until 1963. The criticism that he was copying Messiaen's second mode of limited transposition obviously rankled for he refuted it often. Although the mode is not the intel-lectual property of Messiaen, it has been noted that 'one has the sensation that Messiaen has patented certain modes ... and that to work with them is to run the danger of committing an act of plagia-rism'.[13] In an RTÉ Radio broadcast in 1989 he stated yet again that at the time of his Violin Concerto, op. 36 (i.e. 1953) he was almost completely ignorant of Messiaen's music.[14] The musicologist in him, however, was drawn to outlining the scale and some of its properties.

This he did in his notes for various talks and programme notes about his works. They show that he was clearly aware of the desired tonal ambiguity that his scale generated and he wrote out the 1–2–1 collection bracketing a Dorian scalar section, the intervals of the minor third and the perfect fourth, the inherent structure of minor thirds, and in addition noted how the Phrygian cadence is suggested by the 'tendency to relieve tension by downward semitone'.[15] Joel Lester also points to the latter with reference to Stravinsky's *Symphony of Psalms* noting that 'the octatonic scale beginning E–F and the Phrygian mode on E share five pitch-classes, including the first three scale degrees (E–F–G) allowing smooth transition from one to another'.[16]

Both the diatonic (7–35) and octatonic (8–28) collections have many properties and subsets in common. Both contain all the intervals; however 8–28 contains two diminished sevenths and all the tertian triads (excluding the augmented). The main difference is 8–28's symmetrical axis at the tritone which renders tonic-dominant relationships impossible and its four trichords [0,1,3] with its eight occurrences of the interval class 3. Whereas 8–28 has an interval vector of 448444, 7–35 has a vector 254361 which is one of only four where each entry is unique. Many octatonic pieces can sound vaguely tonal because of the ubiquity of diatonic triads inherent in the collection (see Music Example 1[17]).

In my 1996 article I pointed out that 'in all the quartets, Boydell displays a preference for Model A, the 1–2–1 version so characteristic of Stravinsky's neo-classical period'.[18] Michael Russ suggests that Boydell is drawn to the Model A precisely because he wants the scale that has the major third and fifth of the clear tonic;[19] the notes of this triad are placed on the rhythmically stressed points.

Boydell solved his compositional dilemma by integrating octatonic elements within what was essentially a diatonic framework and it was clearly the properties of the octatonic scale with its minor thirds and alternative 'dominant' on the tritone that attracted him. Never a composer to be tied down by systems however, much of his pitch organisation appears to be guided by instinct and his ear.

One could highlight octatonic passages in his String Trio, op. 21 of 1943–44 where the Model B version (2–1–2) appears in bars 53–54 in the violin (and is then repeated in different registers by the viola and cello respectively); however, as it does not form any part of the motivic material and is more appoggiatura-like, it fails to be of significance. The first crucial work is his String Quartet No. 1, op. 31 of 1949 where he established his compositional language of octatonic and diatonic interaction; it was to do him excellent service for the rest of his career. (see Music Example 2).

This String Quartet opens in the cello with [0,1,3] or pitch class set 3–2 (see Music Example 3), an ordered subset of 8–28 (the viola traces this opening interval enharmonically in bars 11/12). The next three pitches of the octatonic collection are added by the viola in bar 6 (see Music Example 4) thereby producing the octatonic hexachord 6–Z13 which provides the material for all of the opening ten bars. It should be noted that 6–Z13 in unison also opens the third movement. Or is Boydell merely using the minor third as motivic material? The fact that he specifically selects the pitches C♯–F♯ in the first violin part in bars 4 and 5 and reinforces them in the cello part in bars 8 and 9 suggests that he knew exactly what he was doing. Further evidence is provided by his lecture notes where this exact 11 bar passage is outlined (see Music Example 5).

However, the prospect of working out the potential of the octatonic hexachord rigorously did not appear to appeal to him and he took the road of developing the rising minor thirds. These thirds are ubiquitous and of course appear in the interval vector of 8–28 eight times. He returns to an inversion of the opening trichord in bars 156–157 at the end of the movement in bars 155–157.

Joseph Ryan has suggested that Boydell was (perhaps subconsciously) influenced in his First String Quartet of 1949 by Frederick May's String Quartet in C♯ minor (of 1936) citing as evidence the opening trichord in the cello and the affirmative close in C major[20] (May begins with a chromatic linear tetrachord and ends in C♯ major). Boydell himself supplied the following programme note for the Tenth Dublin Festival of Twentieth-Century Music in January 1984: 'The whole Quartet is more or less dominated by a scale consisting of alternate semitones and tones, and the first three notes of this scale (C, C sharp, D sharp) form a germinal theme from which most of the material is derived. There is a second theme with Gregorian characteristics which appears at first aetherially, and later builds up into the climax of the movement.'[21] The passionate prayer in the final section of the orchestral work *Masai Mara*, op. 87 (1988) is apparently built on a metamorphosis of an idea from this first string quartet.[22]

The fact that he was aware of the potential of the octatonic scale is displayed at the beginning of the second movement in bars 1–11 (see Music Example 6) when he states the complete octatonic collection in scalar form, gradually drawn out with obvious parallels to the opening of the final movement of Beethoven's First Symphony.

He appears to begin a similar passage from bar 20 in the *Allegro* but the pitch B which is foreign to the collection starts the move away from it and again the collection is abandoned, this time for diatonic gestures, a canon in G minor beginning at bar 74 in the first violin and viola in bar 75. This was anticipated before in bars 68–70 and it culminates in a quite definite dominant seventh on G at bar 90 on a fermata. Here the juxtaposition of the octatonic and diatonic is quite clear as the cadence is interrupted with a statement of a fugal subject in A minor in unison in the cello (see Music Example 7).

This subject can be divided into two segments revealing the prime form 6–32 answered by 8–23. 6–32 constitutes the first six notes of the major scale (although set here in a minor context) and is one of only four pc sets to have vectors in which each entry is unique. It also has the maximum number of interval class 5, i.e. the perfect 4th (or 5th by complementation). The second half of the subject, 8–23, is stated in scalar form (or perhaps interpreted as three trichords of 3–2?) at the beginning of the countersubject in bar 100 followed by two statements of 4–3.

Boydell is fond of such standard contrapuntal techniques and he uses devices such as inversion, stretto, augmentation and soon to develop his subjects. His Third String Quartet, op. 65 also contains a fugue, also in D minor, in an example of octatonic and diatonic interaction (see Music Example 8).

Boydell is very proud of his quartets stating that 'they are the works I would save if everything else was lost'[23] and indeed goes so far as to describe his Third Quartet as 'an avowal of [his] musical beliefs'.[24] He writes that, at the beginning of this quartet, 'elusive high trills are interrupted by a rapid spikey figure which consists of the germinal series of notes from which most of the music develops'.[25] These trills on G–E–C♯ trace a tritone and form the trichord 3–8 (an octatonic subset). Adding the scalar elements of F and D produces the octatonic subset 5–10 (see Music Example 9).

This is followed by the 'spikey figure', a four-note motif 4–Z15 (see Music Example 10), another subset of 8–28 and one of two all-interval tetrachords. This motif is superimposed onto a D minor triad. Both 5–10 and 4–Z15 together constitute the octatonic heptad 7–31 which can act as a surrogate for the full octatonic collection.[26] All the material here is derived from Collection I. In the opening section, bars 1–27 (see Music Example 11), these two tetrachords are repeated seven times each. The two instances of 4–27 in b. 26 could be expanded into 5–28. The final five notes in the viola must be seen as either 4–28 or 5–31. The section ends in C♯ (as does the quartet) tracing the tritone from the opening G of the first violin to the C♯ of the cello, the C♯ here functioning as a quasi dominant. There follows a complete statement of 7–31, the octatonic heptad in bars 28–29. The final five notes in the first violin spell 5–10 (see Music Example 12). A four-bar passage introduces a flavour of A minor settling on 4–Z29 (b. 34) and A major on 4–18 (b. 36), both octatonic tetra-chords: the all-interval tetrachord 4–Z29 [0,1,3,7] containing a minor triad and 4–18 [0,4,7] containing a major triad (see Music Example 13).

The piece settles again on 4–Z29 in bar 44 (this time with a C minor feel) flanked by occurrences of 4–14, a non-octatonic tetra-chord. Another statement of the octatonic heptad 7–31 appears in bar 56 and the piece progresses utilising 4–27 and 5–10. It is natural enough that complete statements of 7–31 and the 4–Z29 sonorities should appear again in the reprise of material. The first movement (or section) ends on an open C♯ (b. 163–167) and is preceded by two statements of 4–27 and an inversion of the 5–10 material in bars 158–161 from the opening bars of the quartet (see Music Example 14). The entire quartet ends with a unison statement of 5–28 in bar 477 and four bars of unison C♯ (see Music Example 22).

A comparison of his Violin Concerto and the Second String Quartet, op. 44 written within a few years of each other reveals interesting relationships between the pitch class material. The Violin Concerto had its first performance on 1 October 1954 with the soloist Jaroslav Vanacek and the Radio Éireann Orchestra under Milan Horvat. Fleischmann feels that the Violin Concerto 'is proba-bly the best constructed – brittle, energetic, with moments of quiet, lyrical beauty, as in the etherial coda of the Lento'[27] which Boydell admits is very Irish.[28] Boydell begins it with a statement in unison strings and wind of 5–10 (see Music Example 15), an ordered subset and linear pentad of 8–28 and immediately follows it with the quartal (and non-octatonic) sonority 3–9 in the trombones in bars 2–4 (see Music Example 16).

This is followed by the trichordal subsets of 3–2 which leads to the combination of 3–2 and 3–9 in bars 13–15 (see Music Example 17) and repeated, *molto rit*, at the end of the *Rondo* in bars 287–9.

A comparison of this with the opening of the Second String Quartet which begins with the tetrachord [0,1,3,4], 4–3 (as does the *Adagio and Scherzo* for String Quartet, op. 89 of 1991) and a subset of 8–28 shows that he also contrasts it with 3–9 (see Music Example 18).

In his lecture notes on the Second String Quartet he notes his 'obsession with the scale of alternate tones and semitones' and also noted in brackets the 'danger [of] dim[inished] 7ths'.[29] His notes, however, tend to focus on motivic and structural elements, often in Toveyian language. 'The Second Quartet ... was very much influenced by a new-found interest in medieval music. I had discovered the music of Guillaume de Machaut'. Boydell transcribed the opening bars of this quartet as his contribution to *The Whoseday Book (A Millennium Journal)*.[30] It is based on ideas adumbrated in his *Divertimento for Three Music Makers* of 1954.

The *Megalithic Ritual Dances*, op. 38, written in the mid-1950s, also open with 4–3 in the violins (see Music Example 19) and also uses quartal harmony (e.g. 4–26, G–C–B♭–E♭) over bars 127–135.

Octatonic & Quartal Sets	
String Quartet No. 2	4–3 & 3–9
Violin Concerto	4–3 & 3–9
Megalithic Ritual Dances	4–3 & 4–26

The material in the Violin Concerto continues to reveal octatonic, diatonic and quartal interaction. For instance, the solo violin plays 5–23 (a diatonic subset) in bar 92 against ten bars of 4–23 (superimposed fourths F–B♭–E♭–A♭). In fact Boydell finishes the movement on 4–23 (and later the entire concerto). The second movement displays full statements of 8–28, for example in bars 7 and 8 (see Music Example 20).

The third movement also opens with a full statement of 8–28[31] (see Music Example 21). The cadenza is approached with the repeated octatonic sonorities of 5–28 pentachords (bars 158–166). From bars 291 onwards, 8–28 is stated in scalar form over three octaves and 'resolves' on an E (the projected tonal centre of the piece) in bar 294.

Many of his pieces, if not specifically in a key, reflect a focal pitch-class or project a tonal centre and end often in either a unison passage or with a single unison note or diatonic chord. In the first String Quartet, C is a focal pitch-class for much of the piece: the first movement begins and ends on a C, the second movement begins on C and ends with *fff* open C–G–C chords, and the final movement culminates in two crashing C major chords after the same unison octatonic scale which began the movement (see Music Example 22). The two movements of the second Quartet centre around G and E/B respectively whereas the third Quartet clearly resolves on a C♯ repeated in unison twelve times (see Music Example 23). The early String Trio of 1943–44 has a C major feel in many passages and the *Adagio and Scherzo for String Quartet* of 1991 finishes on a unison C. The Violin Concerto centres around E and the early orchestral piece, *In Memoriam Mahatma Gandhi* of 1948 around D♭. The seven pitch-class sets to which ordered segments of 8–28 belong are 7–31, 6–Z13, 6–Z23, 5–10, 4–3, 4–10, and 3–2. The following table indicates the works in which these pcs are used for salient thematic material:

String Quartet No. 1 (1949)	8–28	6–Z13	3–2	
Violin Concerto (1953/54)	8–28	5–10	4–10	3–2
Megalithic Ritual Dances (1956)	4–3			
String Quartet No. 2 (1957)	4–3			
String Quartet No. 3 (1969)	7–31	5–10		

In conclusion, I wish to highlight the question of Boydell's Irishness which has been explored recently by Philip Graydon by examining Aloys Fleischmann's assertion that 'there lies, not far beneath the surface certain individual mannerisms – details of melodic curve, certain tonal progressions – which relate back to Irish folk song, and which stamps the composer's work a part of the Irish tradition, as clearly as that of James Joyce'.[32] Graydon notes Boydell's 'emphatic cosmopolitanism [which] makes instances of the "Irish" note in [his] *oeuvre* all the more subtle and enriching'.[33] Indeed, Boydell admitted in interview with Charles Acton in 1970 that 'there is one particular little figure which keeps cropping up in my music, and I notice it keeps cropping up in Irish folk music. It's completely unconscious, it just happens. I think I use the sort of characteristic Irish melismata unconsciously.'[34] Graydon identifies this in the Violin Concerto in bar 103 of the first movement (see Music Example 24) and also notes in the String Quartet No. 2 in bars 6 – 10, 'a phrase-ending with a definite "Irish" character in its "gapped" sonority' (see Music Example 25) and also notes the 'Irish Melisma' in bar 14 in the cello part.[35]

Much later, however, Boydell stated that he 'always eschewed the idea of writing "Irish" music ... nevertheless the flavour seems to have got under my skin and I think that comes out very much in my violin concerto';[36] and in 1997 he said, 'I have never wanted to use a folk song, but I could not help absorbing folk music'.[37] Other 'Irish' works include his *Shielmartin Suite*, op. 47 (1959), Four Sketches for Two Irish Harps, op. 52 (1962), *Four Yeats Songs*, op. 56 (1966), the choral work *A Terrible Beauty is Born*, op. 59 (1965), *Symphonic Inscapes*, op. 64 (1968) and various film scores such as *The Wooing of Etain*, op. 37 (1954).

BOYDELL – MUSIC EXAMPLES

Music Example 1: Octatonic Collections

Music Example 2: String Quartet No. 1 (bars 1–11)

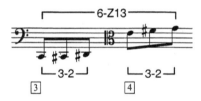

Music Examples 3 & 4: String Quartet No. 1, First Movement (opening)

Music Example 5: From Boydell's Lecture Notes for his String Quarter No. 1

Music Example 6: String Quartet No. 1, Second Movement (bars 1–11)

Music Example 7: String Quartet No. 1, Second Movement (bars 95–100)

Music Example 8: String Quartet No. 3 (bars 310–314)

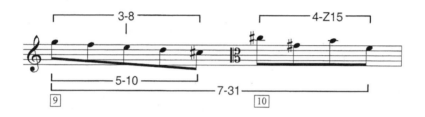

Music Examples 9 & 10: String Quartet No. 3 (opening bars)

Music Example 11: String Quartet No. 3 (bars 1–27)

Music Example 11: Continued

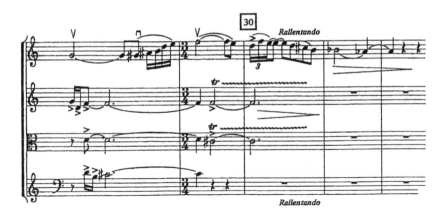

Music Example 12: String Quartet No. 3 (bars 28–32)

Music Example 13: String Quartet No. 3 (bars 33–36)

Music Example 14: String Quartet No. 3 (bars 156–167)

Music Examples 15 & 16: Violin Concerto (opening)

Music Example 17: Violin Concerto, First Movement (bars 13–15) Solo Violin

Music Example 18: String Quartet No. 2, First Movement (bars 1–8)

Music Example 19: Megalithic Ritual Dances (opening)

Music Example 20: Violin Concerto, Second Movement (bars 7 & 8)

Music Example 21: Violin Concerto, Third Movement (opening bars)

Music Example 22: String Quartet No. 1, First Movement (bars 274–278)

Music Example 23: String Quartet No. 3 (bars 477–483)

Music Example 24: Violin Concerto, First Movement (bar 103)

Music Example 25: String Quartet No. 2, First Movement (bars 6–10)

CHAPTER THREE

'Our musical state became refined'[1]: the musicology of Brian Boydell

HARRY WHITE

First, the word 'musicology': Brian Boydell would probably have disdained it. Its connotations of remote scholarship and detached, archival enquiry would have offended his resolutely engaged and pragmatic sense of music history, although as anyone with a passing interest in his work will know, Boydell was no stranger to the archive. On the contrary: he was most at home there. Perhaps 'music history' is a more just description of his research, although that term is troublesome enough too. It is not that Boydell's research interests were confined by his aesthetic sensibility as a composer: it is, rather, that he rarely (if ever) allowed his aesthetics to impinge on his abiding interest in eighteenth-century music in Ireland. The Ireland of Boydell's musical scholarship (there is a satisfactory designation after all), is also difficult to define: words like 'colonial', 'fashionable', 'Gaelic' and 'elegant' pervade his writings with a sense of diffident unease, as if the writer were aware of the ghost of history at his side, but unwilling to admit him onto the page.

What Boydell does accommodate is information: opinion or the interpretation of history is often of secondary concern to him, but information itself, the painstaking recovery of Dublin's musical life in all its plenitude of factual detail, is the crowning merit and purpose of his scholarly work. Perhaps this enduring fascination with the very fabric, the felt life of the profession (or 'trade', to use his own, preferred term) reflects Boydell's early training as a scientist:

verifiable information, the empirical value of documentary evidence, take ascendancy (a predestined pun) over any particular history of ideas. Nevertheless, there *is* an idea which stands behind his work, and it finds expression again and again in Boydell's brilliant recovery of music in eighteenth-century Ireland. I shall identify that idea here as a powerful nostalgia for Ireland's cultural sovereignty in the decades prior to the Act of Union; but in order to realise the implications of this idea, we need to be aware of Boydell's own position as a composer in Ireland in the middle decades of the twentieth century.

I take it that this position is addressed elsewhere in this volume, but my purpose in adverting to it here is to remark the contrast between the deplorable condition of the composer in mid-twentieth-century Ireland and the coherence of music – if only as an 'elegant entertainment' in eighteenth-century Dublin. This contrast repays a moment's further deliberation. The history of art music in Ireland in the twentieth century – of which Boydell's compositions form so distinguished a part – can fairly be characterised as an attempt to redeem music from the burdens of nationalist ideology. The oppressive presence of that ideology, not least after the formation of the Irish Free State in 1922, manifested itself unmistakably in the widespread failure to conceive of original composition in terms other than those which the ethnic repertory proposed. What I have elsewhere described as 'the dutiful presence of the [Irish] air' was ubiquitous in the formative years of Brian Boydell's career as a musician, and the restricted conditions which this servitude implied for art music were widely debated in Irish periodical literature throughout the 1930s and 1940s.[2] This debate need not be rehearsed here; it is sufficient to note that Boydell was among its leading participants, so that his observations on the future of music in Ireland, published in 1951, were informed not only by professional self-awareness and self-interest, but by a more general awareness of the intellectual stagnation and impoverished infrastructures which retarded the condition of music in this period.[3]

Boydell's disavowal, moreover, of the shibboleths of nationalism, together with the admixture of celticism and European (English, German) vocabulary which suffused his compositions, represented a vitally different (but no less committed) image of Ireland to that which the reliance on folksong embodied and drearily perpetuated. If others, by force of circumstance or personality, retreated from this sorry blend of cultural oppression and actual economic hardship, or took sombre refuge in sour polemics, Boydell did otherwise. Perhaps his sheer versatility of mind protected him from the torpor or melancholy deliberations which engulfed composers like Frederick May and even, for a time, Aloys Fleischmann. But whereas Fleischmann's emancipation from this paralysing indifference lay in scholarship and strikingly in an engagement with the traditional repertory that bypassed polemics in favour of German musicology, Boydell proposed a different solution.

Superficially, of course, the parallels between Boydell and Fleischmann are not hard to discover: both occupied university chairs of music; both combined professional and amateur forms of music-making in the wider service of the community; both achieved a considerable reputation for composition; both made vital contributions to musicology in Ireland. Why should it be, then, that one thinks of Boydell first and foremost as a composer, and of Fleischmann as an educator and musicologist? Other than the commonplaces of public perception, the reason may lie in Fleischmann's pursuit of Irish music – extending even to his work on the Celtic Rite – not merely as a species of celticism, but as a positivistic enquiry into the origins and transmission of a specific source or sources of European music (in the widest sense of that designation). Boydell's research, by contrast, is preoccupied not by the provenance of music *per se*, but by the repertory and profession of music in a given, well-defined and limited socio-cultural matrix. Whereas the terminus of Fleischmann's research was to be a *catalogue raisonné* of magisterial authority (*Sources of Irish Traditional Music, c.1600–1855*, New York: Garland, 1998) Boydell's gaze was fixed whole and entire on music as a manifestation of something other than itself. Boydell called this something 'elegant entertainment', but he habitually contextualised this definition as one which 'brings to life the spirit of an age when Dublin's cultural reputation was second only to London's in these islands'.[4] Therein, too, lies the animating spirit of his musical research.

By 'animating spirit' I mean something which is akin to a sense of history. This is something I would wish to acknowledge at the outset, even if Boydell's sense of history – and of eighteenth-century Irish history in particular – should transpire to be different from my own. It is, as I have already inferred, a diffident conception of how things were before the Act of Union, or rather it is an understanding of Irish musical history which foregrounds the idea of a 'golden age' at the expense of more expressly political readings, such as this one: 'The Ascendancy built not only in order to convince themselves that they had arrived, but that they would remain. Insecurity and the England complex would remain with them to the end.'[5]

Brian Boydell does not so much contradict that point of view as leave it to one side. I shall argue here that instead, he construes the musical life of eighteenth-century Dublin in particular as a kind of Ascendancy myth, one which stands in telling opposition to the wretched state of affairs which was art music in Ireland for so much of Boydell's lifetime. I shall argue further that this is a fundamentally Yeatsian reading of cultural history, because it depends – albeit less deliberately than Yeats's view of Ascendancy thinking – upon a contrast between Dublin as the 'second city of the Empire' and Boydell's indictment of 1951, when he wrote that 'music in Ireland … is in a shocking state'.[6] Nevertheless, I would also emphasise that Boydell's sense of history is neither a matter of bad faith nor of naive sentimentality. The powerfully nostalgic condition of his politics does not eclipse a determination to recover as accurately and as factually as he might the surface structure of Dublin's musical life. Evidence precedes explanation in history as in science, and in Boydell's case, the provision, the indispensable recovery of evidence is the objective of almost everything he has written. Boydell is concerned not to discover why the Ascendancy 'built' (or made music, for that matter), but to what extent they built, and how they did so.

*   *   *

The three central texts with which I am primarily concerned in this essay all come close together, and near the end of Boydell's prodigious career as a musician. By their nature, two of them – *A Dublin Musical Calendar, 1700–1760* (1988) and *Rotunda Music in Eighteenth-Century Dublin* (1992) – reflect that long act of recovery from the archive which preoccupied Boydell for thirty years, and in the service of which he sought early retirement as Professor of Music at Trinity College, Dublin, in 1982. The earliest of the three texts, the chapters on 'Music before 1700' and 'Music, 1700–1850' in *A New History of Ireland* (1986), was itself prefigured by a number of smaller writings, notably contributions to learned proceedings (of the

Royal Musical Association [1978–79]), chapters in books (including the first volume of *Irish Musical Studies, Musicology in Ireland* [1990]) and occasional papers. Boydell also edited a series of talks on *Four Centuries of Music in Ireland* for the BBC in 1979 and wrote important articles for *The New Grove Dictionary of Music and Musicians* (1980).[7]

His major work, however, is available in the three texts I have nominated here, which respectively comprise an historical survey, an archival study or catalogue, and a monograph. Taken together, these texts disclose Boydell's concern with the sovereignty of information, a priority that speaks to and redresses the impoverished sense of Ireland's musical past which dominated his youth and early middle age in this strange country.

The chapters on music in *A New History of Ireland* principally attempt two things. One is to offer a coherent narrative of Ireland's musical past; the other is to explain that past in terms of distinguishing between several forms of cultural relativism: Dublin in relation to London, Dublin in relation to Gaelic Ireland, Irish music in relation to Anglo-Irish music. Each of these pairings Boydell acknowledges as problematic, but it is only the first of them that receives his sustained attention. The narrative itself is a skilful concatenation of events and genres, social custom and charitable enterprise, by which the Ascendancy attained a musical sense of itself. But at the outset, Boydell is careful to identify one prevailing caution, even if this is circumscribed by a blithe salute to affluence:

> Dublin society in the eighteenth century, inspired by the fashionable sophistication of a colonial governing class, encouraged and patronised the arts, which were regarded as an essential decoration of elegant living ... In spite of the dramatic development of musical activity in what is often thought of as Dublin's 'golden age', such events as the first performance of Handel's 'Messiah' in 1742 were not characteristic. That an astonishing amount of music was performed, and that many distinguished European musicians came to Ireland and contributed to this activity, is without question. But, with some notable exceptions, the quality of the music presented and the standard of performance, so far as it can be deduced, do not compare favourably with those of the Continent. The provincial cities reflected the standards and taste of the capital, which itself looked to London; and with the exception of the towering genius of Handel, English musical life in the eighteenth century tended to be a rather pale reflection of the European scene, where the glories of the great symphonic style were evolving.[8]

The caveats in this opening paragraph – Dublin's satellite condition *vis-à-vis* London, and London's *vis-à-vis* the continent – prepare the ground for Boydell's systematic disclosure of concert life, the vagaries of individual artists, the production of music in the cathedrals and in Dublin Castle (and the composers associated with these venues), the absence of serious opera, the building of concert rooms and halls, the promotion of music by charitable societies and hospitals, the performance of *Messiah* in this context of charity promotion, the institution of musical academies, the development of open-air concerts (particularly with regard to the Rotunda), the development of the music trade, the presence of visiting or resident musicians including Dubourg, Cousser, Geminiani and Arne, the popularity of ballad opera in mid-century, the growth of Italian opera in the closing decades of the century, and the reception of Gaelic music among the Ascendancy by means of the Belfast Harp Festival. Thereafter, Boydell considers the decline of musical patronage after the Act of Union and the 'profound changes in taste' to be observed especially in theatre audiences after the turn of the century.

It is a richly layered and densely informative chronicle, buttressed by Boydell's primary research which lay a few years from publication, and supported, too, by the work of T.J. Walsh, Aloys Fleischmann, Ita Hogan and Esther Sheldon, among others. Boydell vividly conveys what I have already described as the 'felt life' of music in Dublin, and he intersperses his narrative with amusing anecdotes of rival singers, intemperate *maestri* and the economic and sexual intrigue which is and always has been indigenous to life in the theatre. There is, too, in these chapters a sense of musical development filtering through the social layers of Ascendancy Dublin, from Castle entertainments directed by the master of His Majesty's Music in Ireland to *The Dragon of Wantley* at the theatre in Aungier Street. Dublin's emulation of London – the commonplace understanding of Irish musical life with which Boydell himself begins – is not supervened by this impressive accumulation of detail.

Boydell's reading of music after the Act of Union in *A New History of Ireland* seems to embody a curious contradiction. Here is his opening paragraph on the subject:

> The coincidence of the act of union and the beginning of a new century has provided a dividing-line in Irish history which has tempted many commentators on the cultural scene to oversimplify the transformation from aristocratic patronage of music and

the arts to a broader and more popular support from the middle classes. Although the troubled times around the turn of the century may have acted as a curtain separating the old order from the new, the first quarter of the nineteenth century was really a period of transition from aristocratic patronage to the gradual crystallisation in the second half of the century of largely middle-class support for music in Irish urban society ... The cultural traditions firmly established by the affluent society of the eighteenth century had sufficient strength to survive the withdrawal of aristocratic patronage and become adapted to conditions altered not only by the union but by more profound changes in European society as a whole.[9]

This optimistic reading, however, is strangely contradicted not only by contemporary accounts of musical decline (exemplified by Joseph Cooper Walker's gloomy comments on the state of music in Ireland at the end of the eighteenth century),[10] but more immediately by the impressive reach of Boydell's own research. As he moves away from the eighteenth century, his chronicle registers an unmistakable transition from professional to amateur norms of music, making which argues against just that degree of cultural continuity espoused by Boydell himself. The decline of the Rotunda concerts, the failure to establish even one professional company of singers or instrumentalists in Dublin, the absence of music education on a scale commensurate with the population of the capital and the continued reliance on the sporadic importation of visiting musicians from London are scarcely redressed by the occasional performance of Haydn and Beethoven or isolated tours by Paganini and Liszt.

Indeed the constant mode is secondary: London leads in this narrative, and Dublin follows. Gifted composers like Field and Balfe inevitably forsake this barren terrain for more creative ground abroad, and in the meantime the older models of charity promotion continue to lose ground. By mid-century, we are arrived at a point where concert and operatic life in Dublin is almost wholly dependent upon the foreign tour or visiting company, and the absence of professional infrastructures widens the gap between aspiration and achievement to the extent that Ascendancy forms of patronage look attractive by comparison. Despite the proliferation of amateur societies and associations, the contrast between Dubourg, Cousser, Geminiani and Arne in Dublin before the Act of Union and Cooke, Geary, Logier, Giordani and Rooke after it, could scarcely be more pronounced. One does not have to read between the lines of

Boydell's narrative to propose that art music had become a form of sporadic entertainment and a peripheral force in Irish life as the nineteenth century wore on. While Boydell's responsibility is to show how various (if tenuous) its presence was throughout Irish society as a whole, the record is dismally meagre, especially in terms of original composition.

Given the essentially downward curve of these chapters from *A New History of Ireland*, the book which follows would seem to propose a different reading of history. *A Dublin Musical Calendar, 1700–1760* is a *tour de force*. It makes use of some twelve Dublin newspapers or newsheets of the period, together with various contemporary and modern secondary sources, to document – day by day where possible – every significant musical event which took place in Dublin between 1700 and 1760. Six appendices to the calendar offer supplementary material on the Dublin music trade (music shops, instrument makers, publishers, printers and music sellers), on venues for music in Dublin, on 'societies and charitable bodies connected with music in Dublin', on composers, performers and other musical personalia, on music performed or published in Dublin (in the form of an index), and, finally, on the principal events, personalities and venues featured in each concert season of the period (this last appendix effectively constitutes a summary of the calendar itself). The composite picture of Dublin musical life which the calendar affords is a complex one, which includes not only theatrical music (excluding *opera seria*) but also instrumental genres (e.g. Italianate concertos) and church music, annual performances occasioned by state celebrations, and musical events expressly commissioned in aid of charitable causes (most typically the support of hospitals and infirmaries).

Boydell's work is especially useful, then, in three respects. Firstly, it allows us to trace the Dublin careers of foreign-born or visiting composers whose activities comprise the proper context in which Handel's visit to Dublin should be seen. The contributions of Arne, Cousser, Dubourg, Geminiani, Niccolò Pasquali and the Roseingrave family are as fully disclosed by Boydell as contemporary records will allow. The composers associated with ballad opera comprise a separate group, insofar as most of them – with the sovereign exception of Arne – tend to be associated with no other musical genre. The impact of Handel's music both during and after his stay in the city can thereby be compared by means of this *Calendar* with that of his composer-colleagues in Dublin. Beyond the sphere of ballad opera, Boydell's research repeatedly affirms a preference for Handel (especially in oratorio and church music) which endured long after 1742. The predominance of *Acis* and the oratorios, season after season and year after year is such that no other composer begins to rival Handel's popularity in the middle decades of the century. Ballad opera and Handel oratorio would seem to determine the polar extremes of Ascendancy musical taste.[11]

Secondly, Boydell offers detailed information on a host of societies and charitable bodies by which music was promoted and performed in Dublin. Such information allows us to distinguish the Dublin musical scene from that of London in one major respect: in London, music was generally in the hands of private enterprise or the aristocracy. In Dublin, it was primarily a means of supporting the public good. This distinction partly explains the success Handel enjoyed with *Messiah* in Dublin by comparison with its subsequent (initial) failure in London. Although the *Calendar* reminds us that Handel's visit was largely to his own profit, the use of *Messiah* (and many other works following his departure) for the promotion of charity in Dublin cannot be too strongly contrasted with the promotion of music in London. One might suggest, indeed, that charity provided the Ascendancy with its outward *raison d'être* for the patronage of high forms of musical culture.

Finally, Boydell clarifies the locations of public (and occasionally private) musical performance and establishes an authoritative list of commercial and non-commercial, indoor and outdoor venues, including churches, theatres and concert halls, together with information as to the length of their use and the principal recurring events associated with each location.

And events do strikingly recur. This would appear to be the determining factor of Dublin musical life in the first six decades of the eighteenth century. Boydell's astounding command of detail begs several questions, chief among them, why it was that so little music was written for Dublin (rather than for London or elsewhere) in spite of this plenitude of performance. Other than *Messiah* (which seems to be the exception that proves the general rule) and a succession of strictly routine birthday odes for the reigning monarch (commissioned from Cousser and Dubourg in the main), the *Calendar* offers no evidence whatever of a freshly composed piece expressly intended for Dublin. In terms of original composition, and against the grain of contemporary musical practice elsewhere in Europe, we witness a musical life being led at second hand. It may be significant that the Ascendancy preferred matters thus, especially if we admit Roy Foster's formulation of 'insecurity and the England-complex' into the equation of musical life in Dublin. And having no music of its own to bequeath, as it were, to succeeding generations of musicians and composers, the Ascendancy left little behind except the long-formed habit of importing the taste, manner and substantive decorum of English musical practice. With the sovereign exception of *opera seria* (itself a waning force in London by the early 1730s), the musical relationship between London and Dublin is an emulative one in the period covered by Boydell's research.

Rotunda Music in Eighteenth-Century Dublin sustains this impression of a borrowed musical existence. In this book, Boydell devotes his attention to a vital subset of Irish musical life, the virtually unbroken series of concerts organised for the benefit of the Dublin Lying-in Hospital (afterwards known as the Rotunda), which began in 1749 and lasted until 1791. Boydell makes available much archival material of the first importance (in particular, the information on musical events contained in the Rotunda Hospital register for the period 1760–84), and he chronicles in detail the immediate circumstances which brought this series of concerts into being, together with its subsequent expansion and decline.

By comparison with the *Calendar, Rotunda Music in Eighteenth-Century Dublin* is somewhat less formal in demeanour. Here, Boydell allows himself space not only to narrate the history of the concert series itself but also to conjecture upon those details of management, repertory, financial planning and musical personnel which comprise the bulk of material presented in the book's five appendices. Boydell draws upon these sources for the structural foundation of the main text, nine chapters which taken together realise his ambition to provide a narrative which is 'readable and entertaining'. These chapters relate in turn the initial efforts of Bartholomew Mosse, founder and first master of the Rotunda, to promote music as a means of raising funds and to secure for this purpose a permanent venue immediately adjacent to the hospital itself (i.e. the gardens which he laid out in Great Britain Street). Boydell also examines the careers of those singers who contributed so decisively to the success of the series; he surveys the design and construction of the Rotunda concert room (opened in 1767, some eight years after Mosse's death) and he considers the development of the summer concerts in particular as 'the plateau of popular and financial success' which the series achieved under Thomas Pinto, an English musician of Italian extraction whose career ended somewhat abruptly in Dublin. Boydell then examines the decline of the series which ensued after 1782, the final year of Pinto's association with the hospital (he died in 1783). The closing chapter concerns the actual music given during the entire period, insofar as this repertory reflects a development of musical taste over a period of forty years.

Each of these chapters affords a multiplicity of insights into Ascendancy musical culture which Boydell reinforces by means of learned speculation and useful comparison with music during the same period in London. In socio-musical terms, one could suggest that Mosse not only sustained the Ascendancy habit of emulating British taste and recreational habit in his successful advocation of a concert series to be held through five summer months in a 'pleasure garden' (modelled on Vauxhall), he also cultivated this idea expressly for the purpose of supporting his hospital. In doing so, Mosse perpetuated the typically Irish association between public music and charitable enterprise by means of a characteristically English proto-type. The Rotunda gardens and even the concert room itself were wholly indebted to London models (such as Vauxhall, Ranelagh and Marylebone), but the motivation of such long-term charitable support was of special relevance to conditions of musical perform-ance in Dublin.

In other respects also, Boydell's Dublin–London comparisons illuminate significant differences between the sociology of musical life in both cities, notwithstanding the virtually absolute dependence of Dublin upon artistic personnel from London (or indirectly from the Continent). The sense of Dublin, indeed, as a harbour of safe refuge for debt-ridden conductors, instrumentalists and singers, is one which is fortified by Boydell's painstaking research. Boydell's asides on the behaviour of audiences, on the precarious conditions of employment and on the cult of the performer in both cities are likewise instructive, if necessarily inconclusive. Boydell's chapter on women singers at the Rotunda (with the Joycean title 'The Sirens') is a compelling admixture of archival exactitude, informed estimations and original commentary which collectively addresses the fees paid to artists, the sexual vulnerability and exploitation of women engaged in any form of theatrical or operatic employment and the

pervasive and glamorous appeal of sexual scandal. A reputation for
les liaisons dangereuses hugely enhanced the drawing-power of
singers at the Rotunda and elsewhere. Women artists engaged for
long winter seasons of opera in Dublin were frequently responsible
for a sudden upsurge in receipts when they sang at the summer
concerts in Great Britain Street. And the repertory which they
performed there, as Boydell's tables illustrate, was directly from the
opera house: songs from Thomas Arne's *Artaxerxes*, *Love in a Village*
and *Comus* are among those given by the wonderful Anne Catley
when she sang at the Rotunda in the 1770s. In her case at any rate,
the author enthusiastically conveys the impression of a singer whose
artistic prowess and physical beauty were matched by a 'warm-
hearted nature and generous concern for charity'.

Although Boydell's final chapter provides a review of the 'general
trends shown in the choice of music performed during the four
decades of concerts in aid of the Lying-in Hospital in Dublin', the
book as a whole is characteristically more oriented towards the
performance of music than the music itself. The latter is undoubtedly
addressed insofar as hospital records and newspaper advertisements
permit the author to draw up documentary tables of programmes
and classifications of style (as in 'Music appealing to Popular Taste
and Loyalist Sentiments in the 1780s'). He also surveys the inclusion
of traditional airs performed and/or incorporated within instrumental concertos intermittently between 1749 and 1787. Likewise,
Appendix I, 'Analysis of Music Performed, 1771–1791', summarises
the kind of music given at these concerts in the last two decades of
the series. This last confirms Boydell's point about changes in musical
taste, insofar as the shift away from Handel towards Haydn (and his
contemporaries) reflects Dublin's absorption of the classical style and
the gradual loss of baroque musical practice there.[12]

* * *

> Music history is possible only insofar as the historian is able to
> show the place of individual works in history by revealing the
> history contained within works themselves, that is, by the reading
> the historical nature of works from their internal constitution.[13]

Leo Treitler's prescriptive interpretation of what constitutes music
history is part of a wider debate on the nature of the discipline,

especially as to the conflict between the autonomy of the artwork and its functional status in a given historical context.[14] This conflict is variously rehearsed and voiced, but underlying it is an assumption that the relationship between individual artworks and the context from which they emerge is an undeniable one, however problematic that relationship may appear. Put plainly, the musical artwork is always assumed to be indigenous to its context. However fractious the dispute as to whether or not Bach 'intended to compose musical works',[15] no one can dispute that he wrote them in a socio-cultural environment which was at least partly responsible for their shape and form. The development of genre itself (as in opera, cantata, concerto, and so on) is partly and irreducibly a matter of contextual growth, expressive of that synthesis of political and cultural stability from which the European art tradition emerges. If there is a vital difference between individual approaches to genre, as in the difference between Haydn's 104 symphonies and Beethoven's nine or ten essays in this genre, it is a difference mediated by shifts in political and social history, which in this case might be summarised as the implications for music before and after the French Revolution.

There is, too, a pattern of convention, revolution and reception in European art music by which individual acts of musical imagination either conform to cultural norms or defy them: in either case their reception is critically defined by the relationship of these individual acts to the socio-cultural milieu from which they emerge. More locally, we can suggest that in the eighteenth century, music consolidates its position as an expression of political and economic order, notwithstanding the possibility that individual works entail a critique of that order, as (once again) is the case with certain of Bach's cantatas. Indeed Bach's virtually autistic engagement with counterpoint itself comprises a retreat from and an acknowledgement of socio-musical conventions, insofar as the extremity of his musical imagination nevertheless relies on a discourse which is 'universally' understood: that is precisely why Bach's critics condemned his musical style as a wayward and vehemently complex deployment of that discourse.[16]

With Handel, too, there is an evident tension between the claims of imagination, and the composer's obligations to convention and the public discourse of musical style. The plainest manifestation of that tension in his case is surely the dysfunctional status of *opera seria* in London, insofar as Handel's persistence with the genre led to near bankruptcy and ruin. But Handel did not repine: indeed he did not have to do so. His discovery of English oratorio – itself a synthesis *par excellence* of Anglican church music, English bourgeois taste and the strong, narrative line of Italian opera – is a classic instance of that vital accommodation between the individual imagination and its context which guarantees the cultural pre-eminence of musical discourse.

Handel's oratorios are in significant measure (and often explicitly) public celebrations of victory over the Jacobite cause in Hanoverian England. They are underwritten by a political consensus which admits the Bible as the precedent and moral source of Protestant England. However masterly as individual or autonomous artworks, they grow in the soil of English sovereignty. They belong – at least in the first instance – to England. But if the Hanoverian Succession admitted England to the musical resources of continental Europe (not least in the person of Handel himself), the precedent and achievement of Purcell, to say nothing of the wider traditions of Elizabethan and early baroque English music, prove the long-established foundation of art music as a stable resource in England's projection of itself.

This conjunction of public resource and private imagination is not the norm in the Ireland of Brian Boydell's research. But we do find it unmistakably registered in Handel's Dublin sojourn. Its absence otherwise makes Handel's presence in Irish musical affairs all the more powerful both literally and figuratively. I have suggested elsewhere that Handel's music afforded the Ascendancy a sense of itself – a suggestion which is borne out by the prodigious evidence of Boydell's research: charity performance after charity performance of his music is there to support it.[17] In passing, it is useful to observe that the association drawn between Handel's music and the public good was not an invention of Victorian sententiousness but an idea which originated in Ascendancy musical culture itself.[18]

However, this culture was a borrowed one. Another, less charitable paradigm would be to describe it as an imposed culture, like the polity and social systems which it serviced. Handel's famous description of 'that polite and generous nation' self-evidently denotes a society remote from the vast majority of people living in Ireland – or even in Dublin, for that matter. Roy Foster remarks that 'Ascendancy life in Dublin was not notably "cultured"; it was, for instance, largely undistinguished by musical achievements or serious patronage.

Handel's celebrated premiere of *Messiah* on 13 April 1742, is, in fact, an outstanding exception to the general rule.'[19] In the light of Boydell's research, this judgement requires a significant degree of modification. We might say that Ascendancy life in Dublin was musically cultured, but only in the sense that it borrowed, freely and brilliantly, those elements of English musical culture which sustained its own rationalisation of great music in the service of public well-being. Consider, however, Walker's commentary on the state of music in Dublin during the eighteenth century:

> Soon as the Hanoverian Succession was firmly established, the Gates of the Temple of Janus were closed in both Kingdoms. ... The English now pursued with ardour the cultivation of the fine Arts: the Irish crept slowly after. Both vocal and instrumental musicians were brought, at an enormous expence, from Italy to London; and the Italian music began to reign with despotic sway in that great city. ... Its influence spread so wide, that it reached these shores. Our musical state became refined and our sweet melodies and native musicians fell into disrepute ... But alas! in proportion as our musical taste is rectified, the pleasure we derive from pure melody is lessened. This refinement may be said to remove the ear so far from the heart ... that the essence of music (an appellation by which melody deserves to be distinguished) cannot reach it. Nor is it necessary in this age, that the ear and heart should be closely connected. For modern music is calculated only to display the brilliant execution of the performer, and to occasion a gentle titillation in the organ of hearing ... Music was now the rage. Italian Singers were invited over, and the fair Dames of Ireland learned to expire at an Opera ... Concerts were the favourite amusements in the houses of the Nobility and Gentry, and Musical Societies were formed in all the great towns of the Kingdom. In a word, every knee was bowed to St Cecilia. But the Saint was not to enjoy this homage long. In the Rotunda, indeed, her Votaries sacrificed to her for a few years. But Politics, Gaming and every species of Dissipation have so blunted the finer feelings of their souls, that their warm Devotion has at length degenerated into cold Neglect. Concerts, it is true, are held there every Summer, but they are little attended to. Music, however, is sometimes the subject of conversation amongst us, and is still cultivated by a few; but it is no longer a favourite topic, nor a favourite study.[20]

I quote Walker at length here because his commentary encompasses just that period which has been the focus of Boydell's research. It is an interesting passage, because it affords us a contemporary gloss

(1786) on eighteenth-century musical life in Dublin which closely parallels Boydell's reading, some two centuries afterwards. Like Boydell, Walker is alive to the borrowed status of music in Dublin and to the golden age represented by Handel's visit. But his comments are clearly ambiguous, and although they embrace the refinement of musical taste which this golden age brought in its wake, they are explicitly critical in one respect. Walker's discrimination between the artificial status of Italian music and the natural reach of melody is, at the last, a discrimination between art music and the ethnic repertory, a discrimination voiced more explicitly elsewhere.

In this paragraph, moreover, his chronicle implies a degeneration of musical taste which is connected to its status as a superficial adornment, doomed to give way to other pleasures rather than assert itself as an 'essential' expression of nature. His attempt to distinguish between two kinds of music in Ireland, and his aesthetic discriminations in favour of the ethnic repertory as against the imported artifices of the Ascendancy, intimate the crisis and dislocation of music as a force in Irish cultural life. From the high noon of the *Messiah* premiere to the decline of the Rotunda concerts, the very concept of music is, in Walker's view, under duress. All I would add to his reading in the context of Boydell's research is that the failure to produce art works of significance from within Ireland's musically impoverished infrastructures confirms both Walker's pessimism and the absence of musical discussion or analysis from Boydell's writings.

This absence returns us to the outset, and to the suggestion that Boydell's musical research signifies a Yeatsian reading of history. Seamus Deane has argued that Yeats energetically misconstrued the Ascendancy in order to reconstruct an image of the past which would link together the imaginative energies of Gaelic culture and that pantheon of eighteenth-century Anglo-Irish writers, including Burke, Swift, Goldsmith and Sheridan.[21] Deane calls this image an 'historical fiction', and it is certainly not my argument to extend the same gloss to Boydell's research. But I would contend that *A Dublin Musical Calendar* in particular, does confer a certain coherence, a rigorous chronicle of evidence and explanation, upon the hitherto fragmented history of music in Ireland. It is this coherence which stands in ironic opposition to the depleted state of music in Ireland for much of the twentieth century, and especially during the years of Boydell's first maturity as a composer. Moreover, the model of research which

Boydell espoused in this book and elsewhere supervenes the apparent impasse of contemplating a musical history with almost no music of its own. Deprived of the empirical foundations so sturdily provided by Brian Boydell, the cultural history of music in Ireland would lose much of its authority.

CHAPTER FOUR

An interview with Brian Boydell

MICHAEL TAYLOR

In March and April 1989 I conducted an interview with Brian Boydell, just before the first performance of what was to be his last orchestral work, *Masai Mara*. Our discussions (which took place in his room in Trinity College Dublin) extended over three sessions, the tapes of which were transcribed but never edited. The projected publication failed to materialise, and the tapes and transcripts were put aside. When a *Festschrift* was mooted to celebrate his eightieth birthday, the interview seemed an obvious candidate for inclusion, although the inevitable delays have meant that this is, instead, a memorial volume. When the material was located and examined the tape of the third part of the interview was found to be missing (as were all the computer files), although the uncorrected transcript was extant. The remaining tapes were transferred to compact disc and the whole retranscribed; a total of approximately 31,000 words resulted, from which the present text has been edited down to slightly less than half of the original. In making the choice of what to include I have tried to allow Brian Boydell to speak for himself wherever possible, and to this end I have followed the practice outlined by David Sylvester in the Preface to his interviews with the painter Francis Bacon:[1]

> ... since the editing has been designed to present Bacon's thoughts clearly and economically – not to provide some sort of abbreviated record of how the taped sessions happened to develop – the sequence in which things were said has been drasti-

cally rearranged. Each of the interviews ... has been constructed from transcripts of two or more sessions, and paragraphs in these montages sometimes combine things said on two or three different days quite widely separated in time. In order to prevent the montage from looking like a montage, many of the questions have been recast or simply fabricated. The aim has been to seam together a more concise and coherent argument than ever came about when we were talking, without making it so coherent as to lose the fluid, spontaneous flavour of talk.

Our second and third sessions often revisited topics discussed in the first, to correct misapprehension or to elaborate points. Where it seemed appropriate I have incorporated this material into that of the first part, although some small repetitions remain. Occasionally he asked that an opinion or comment not be published, and I have respected his wishes each time. Where the inevitable slips of memory occur I have silently corrected them, even though I suspect that he would have enjoyed his transposition of Mosolov into Molotov.

MT   A large amount of your education took place in England: you studied natural sciences at Cambridge and then music. Why did you decide to go to Cambridge?

BB   That goes back quite a long way. First of all, in the Anglo-Irish community, the Ascendancy, if you like, from which I came, it was the done thing for gentlemen to send their children to school in England to get rid of the terrible Irish accent. That was the general background, and after I had been to school for a short time here in Ireland, I was sent to a very scholastic prep school, the Dragon School, in Oxford, when I was only nine years old. At the Dragon School I was quite a promising musician. With a couple of friends of mine we formed what we called a jazz band in which we used to play things like 'It ain't going to rain no more, no more'. I started writing a few things of my own but they were not that style, and we played them.

MT   Was that the first time that you had a composition performed?

BB   The very first thing I ever remember having performed by other people was in Switzerland. We were brought winter sporting and the hotel had a tea-time orchestra, a piano trio, and I wrote a short piece for them. They were awfully nice about it; I wrote a low B flat for the cello and he so kindly pointed out that this was not on the instrument. I had the desire to do things like that and was enormously interested in music. After the Dragon School I was meant to go to Winchester, I think very largely because my mother was rather an intellectual snob, and, as it was the brainiest of all the public schools, to have a Winchester scholarship was the top of the world for her. My father had a thing about manners and the motto of Winchester was 'Manners maketh man', so he thought that was a very good thing, too. When he interviewed my future housemaster the housemaster was so rude to him that he took my name off the list. The big change came when I went to Rugby instead, where the Director of Music was a man called Kenneth Stubbs. He had an enormous personality through which he was able to convey his enthusiasm for music. He more or less took me under his wing, and I became enormously keen, finally graduated to winning the prize for the best pianist in the school, and played one of the Rachmaninov and the Grieg concertos with the school orchestra. He then suggested that it might be a good idea to teach me harmony and so I had private lessons with him at his house.

MT   Your father supported all this?

BB   I never had a great deal of contact with my father. I think it was rather sad in a way. He was a very strict man who thought it was his duty to bring me up well. The result was that he behaved more or less like a schoolmaster and we never had much human contact. I was always getting into trouble for all sorts of things which were not the right thing to do, being scolded for this, and Stubbs became a father figure to me, and had an enormous influence on my life, so that music became my greatest interest at that time. As well as learning harmony I started writing quite a lot of music at Rugby. I wrote two organ sonatas, and a song, 'Wild Geese', which, curiously enough, is still all right, I think. It was a setting of a poem by the headmaster, and, while I am still not ashamed of it, I remember setting another poem by him called 'Communion' and that is the most ghastly rubbish you have ever seen. I found it the other day; a terrible drippy, sentimental, Ketèlbey-type[2] of thing. I went through a period of religious mania when I was about fifteen and I suppose it belongs to that time.

MT   When did your interest in science begin?

BB   At the age of about eight, when I was given a chemistry set, I became enormously keen on experimental chemistry, it was my hobby. I set up my own laboratory at home and I spent all my pocket money on chemicals. A great influence was William Fearon, Professor of Biochemistry in Trinity, who was one of the last great polymaths. He wrote plays for the Abbey, collected vintage motorcars, and one of his hobbies was building organs. He had written a pantomime song at the age of ten, for which he refused five pounds, because he thought he would make his fortune, and he was a tremendous influence, making me very interested in science as well as encouraging the musical side. The two things were running parallel all the time; I was doing pretty well in science at Rugby and very much leading in music. I then won a Choral Exhibition to Clare College, Cambridge. I was examined by Boris Ord[3] who spotted my interest in Delius when I showed him the variations I had written for piano on an Irish tune. I knew Delius' music through gramophone records, and I was very excited by the sounds he made.

MT   Had you always collected records?

BB   I collected gramophone records when I was at Rugby. I had a gramophone in my study and, in those days, one did not come across contemporary music. Things were so different. There were very few records available but I got hold of Debussy's String Quartet which was an absolute revelation to me, I was so excited by it. Ernst Bloch's first String Quartet also had a very big influence on me, because he found a type of romanticism that was not nineteenth-century and that did not have that slightly worn-out flavour to it. In fact, anything that had a fresh note to it I cottoned-on to and I suppose my early enthusiasms happened just because I happened to come across one particular person who was available on a gramophone record. There was no opportunity of making your choice of which of the modern composers interested you most, because you hardly heard any. It was only by these means that you could hear such things, unless you lived in London.

MT   What did you do between leaving school and going up to Cambridge?

BB   I had six months in Heidelberg from the end of the Easter term in 1935 until August. I learnt German very quickly (that was the chief idea), and had piano lessons with one of the up-and-coming pianists who became a great Nazi party member after-wards. I was loosely attached to the university, only loosely because I enrolled in the Protestant Church Music Institute, to get organ lessons from a man who was supposedly the best organist in Southern Germany. I had a very interesting time with him. I was introduced to the sound of a Baroque organ which delighted me, having been used to the English roast-beef type at Rugby. That is when the dam broke because the richness of musical life in Germany then was quite amazing. I was able to take the train and attend the *Ring* three times through at Mannheim for a shilling an opera with a student card. And I became Wagner-mad, much to the disgust of my teacher, the old Professor in whose house I was living. He disapproved of the literary quality of Wagner's prose and I insisted on studying all the libretti of the Wagner operas, particularly the *Ring*, and he did not like that at all. But, I became soaked in Wagner and then went to the Munich festi-val, which ran alternately with Bayreuth (and was then of a rather higher standard), where I heard *Tristan, Die Meistersinger von Nürnberg* and *Parsifal* for the first time. I never went to bed the night after *Tristan*, just walking around the place dreaming about this marvellous music. I was overwhelmed by Wagner. I met Richard Strauss for the first time and was lucky enough to see a production of *Die Frau ohne Schatten* which is so complicated to stage that it is hardly done anywhere: sixteen-foot fountains on the stage lit up with coloured lights. Marvellous with the music; it worked extremely well. I went to a Mozart opera, *Die Zauberflöte*, and I was disgusted with it. I thought it was silly. I mean it is funny the way you just miss the point of something. But actually, I think, on the whole, Mozart is a very adult taste, either a terri-bly primitive one or a very adult one.

MT   How did you continue your musical studies when you went to Cambridge?

BB   I was still enormously keen on science but felt more and more drawn to music, and I became very active in the College Music Society, finally more or less running it. I spent far more time at music than I did at science. Because I had my own laboratory at home, I did all my scientific work during the vacation, one of the reasons being the lectures were so appalling that it was far better to read the books. As you did not have to go to lectures in Cambridge I used to pop across the road from the science block to the Music School and listen to Edward Dent, and I became completely involved with all the musicians. I became active too in the Cambridge University Music Society and the Music Club in which members of the committee arranged concerts alternately. At the same time I was involved with the Chapel Choir, singing in it as part of my duty, having singing lessons, and then a pupil of Solomon[4] came down from London each week to give me a lesson, by special arrangement with my father figure, Kenneth Stubbs. He put me through the very stiff technical training of the Solomon school, which, in the end, I think, broke my spirit. He was so exacting in perfection that I lost my nerve and could not play the keyboard in public without going to pieces. Some time later, when I went to the Royal College, I gave up the piano as a virtuoso instrument, switching over to other things, and I am very glad I did.

MT   How did the move into an 'official' music course happen?

BB   At Cambridge I was acquiring a scientific education because my father wanted me to go into the family business, which was malting, mainly for Guinness, and I was very interested in doing research in the area of malt-biochemistry, biochemistry being one of my chief subjects. When it came towards the end of my time at Cambridge I managed to get a first class degree in the Natural Science Tripos, my father agreed to give me a period at the Royal College of Music, and I remember throwing my slide-rule into the back of the car after I had finished my last exam thinking that I would never bother with it again. I thought I had really made the break; this was what I wanted to do.

MT   That must have been a stimulating move for you.

BB   I had a flat in London, where one was open to all the things going on in the city, for example, the Sibelius Festival, and I went Sibelius mad. There were concerts pretty regularly and there was a group of us who got turned completely upside down: we would get up about four o'clock, have breakfast and then go off to the concert and then we would come home at about midnight and talk about the music all night, and go to bed about ten o'clock the next morning. We were totally wrapped up in our own enthusiasms, and terribly intense and excited about it all. The symphonies, the Violin Concerto and quite a good block of the tone poems were received with great enthusiasm. It was Beecham conducting most of them I think. About this time I came across Berg. *Wozzeck* had not yet been done in London, but the pieces from the opera had been broadcast by the BBC. Going to concerts those days in London was expensive and my father kept me on a very slender allowance. So, this friend of mine and I, who shared the flat, decided the best thing to do was only to go to concerts which were not broadcast, because otherwise we would listen on the radio. But we did attend the whole Toscanini Festival, which provided an opportunity of hearing somebody who really could produce an electric sound from an orchestra. I often look back on Toscanini's readings of Beethoven (because they were mostly Beethoven concerts) and I do not think I would approve of them now, but they certainly were electric and so exciting. I particularly remember his Seventh: it lifted one right outside this world.

MT   What did you study at the College?

BB   Life at the Royal College was very active and this is where I studied composition, nominally with Patrick Hadley.[5] I took up the oboe, which I learnt from a dear old man with a walrus moustache, who used to play in Henry Wood's orchestra, one of the old style orchestral instrumentalists. Remember, Goossens[6] was probably the first gentleman to become an orchestral player. The College was marvellous because it really provided a good musical education; as a background you attended lectures in the history of music. They were pretty staid but at least they introduced you to some ideas, an outline. And they had dictation classes, which I found the most valuable thing I ever did and they really were tough. I took piano as well, having moved from the Solomon man to Angus Morrison. I became enormously fond of Patrick Hadley; he was a great friend of mine later on. A rather interesting person, both he and Herbert Howells[7] (with whom I also had lessons) represent a type of English composer who everyone thought was going to make it and be a great composer but somehow they never did.

MT   Why do you think this was the case with Hadley?

BB   Some of Patrick Hadley's music is extremely good, but not quite good enough to break through, and it makes you think about the whole business of who does break through. How far is it due to publicity from a publisher that a composer becomes successful, or how far is it that their music really is the best? It is a thing I often wonder about, particularly in relation to contemporary Irish music, where there is no publishing house, no recording company, and there is little money to do things. I often wonder would contemporary Irish music have a bigger name if the whole business of publicity and plugging and selling did not come into the game. Hadley was sometimes indisposed but he always had this arrangement with his friend Howells that Herbert would take his pupils when he was not in, and as a result of this I think I had the best compositional lesson that I have ever had in my life. I had written a song, I think it was a rather soppy sentimental song I had written for a girlfriend I had just discovered, and I brought it in to Paddy Hadley who looked at it and he said 'that's a very crawly bass, let's have some decent manly jumps here', and he sketched out the way that he would like the bass to go, 'go away and write it again'. So I went off and I rewrote the thing with some 'decent manly jumps' in the bass, and the next week, as Paddy was indisposed, I went to Herbert Howells and brought him this song, and he said 'that's a very angular bass there, don't you think a nice chromatic falling theme would be rather nice? Go away, rewrite that, take out all that awful angular stuff,' and I think it was that experience that taught me that the only way you can learn composition is through self-criticism. I find it awfully hard, in fact, I always refuse, to teach composition because I know that I am too much influenced by the things that I like, and that people can see straight through me when I just respect the things that I do not like. One has to be frightfully objective and broad-minded when judging people's work for examinations and say 'well I think that's an absolutely horrible noise but I can see it is well done'. But this business of self-criticism is really the only thing you can teach, apart from the fundamental things which one must learn anyway.

MT   So what, apart from self-criticism, would you say you learnt from Hadley and Howells?

BB   I think what one learnt is the fact that you had to write things and bring them to have them criticised. It made you work.

They would say, for instance, write a song to show me how you can manage a pedal point and that would make you explore the possibilities of the pedal point and then the comments would be useful, but it really was their comments and the challenge of having to do the thing that made you think for yourself and made you critical of the result you had produced. A great friend of mine studied with Vaughan Williams, and I offered to play a piece he had written for cor anglais at his lesson. I had the most delightful time, playing this piece and hearing Vaughan Williams criticising and talking about it.

MT Were Hadley and Howells sympathetic to the Sibelian and Bergian influences which, presumably, were appearing in what you wrote?

BB I do not remember them commenting very much on things like that. They were, both of them, I think, very broad-minded, and, if you did something rather strange, they might say 'now are you sure, do you really like that?' Howells might say, 'I would say that that comes as too much of a jerk in the harmonies at that point having that horrible discord there.' In fact it was more making you think about it rather than saying it was bad. I find it awfully hard to remember precisely very much more except the general feeling that to be bound up in music was terribly exciting, you were set these things to do, you faced the challenge and came out the other end with a sense of self-criticism.

MT How much music by Schoenberg, Berg and Webern was being played in London at this time?

BB Very little. I would say I only came across it in our contemporary music club in the College. I remember a frightfully intense young gentleman with pebble-spectacles playing the Webern pieces for cello and piano[8] with somebody who had just come from Austria. And I remember, that was too much for me. I thought that was really rather funny actually, because of the whole set-up; they were so earnest. I never really took to either Schoenberg or Webern: it is the romantic side of Berg that attracted me. Charles Lynch[9] had a great name in London as one of the best exponents of Schoenberg shortly before the war. We could never persuade him to do that over here, because he was a person who could only play in front of an audience who appreciated what he was doing, and it was very hard to find such an audience here, being such a small country.

MT You studied singing in London, too.

BB I studied singing very seriously indeed with a marvellous tutor who dealt entirely with voice production. I was sent to her by Agnes Nichols – Lady Harty – who was one of the great oratorio sopranos at the time. I wanted lessons from her, I knew her actually, and after she heard me sing she said 'you haven't the faintest idea how to sing, go and learn how to sing before you come to me'. She sent me off to Louise Trenton, who was a marvellous woman. You had a lesson every day; the whole thing was that you had to keep at it. So I knew a lot about voice production, having gone through the mill with her, and when I set up here teaching voice production nobody in Dublin was actually teaching it.

MT This was after your return to Ireland following the outbreak of war. Would you have stayed had war not broken out?

BB That is awfully hard to say. I am very glad it did force me back in many ways. I went to the Royal College in autumn 1938, and the following year war broke out, which interrupted my time there. I then came back to Ireland and my father put me to work in the family business as a chemist. I became rather disillusioned with that after some time and got a job teaching painting at a school here, and set up as a teacher of vocal production. Gradually I established myself enough to be able to get out of the malting firm and become a full-time professional musician, but it was a struggle in the beginning. I had become a very strong pacifist very early on in my career, much earlier than many people normally do perhaps. I was revolted by the whole attitude of the Officer Training Corps at Rugby, and my first reaction there was to be rather a wild rebel and try and disrupt the whole thing. In the end I resigned saying I did not approve of the thing at all. And that gave me the great opportunity: I had to work. I enjoyed working at chemistry, so I spent the afternoon in the labs doing experimental chemistry. When the war broke out the natural thing was to come back here because Ireland was neutral. On the other hand, I am aware of the fact that unlike Britten, who was slightly older than me, and Tippett (who I had met in musical circles in London) I was never put to the test as they were, and I regret that. It was too easy even though my father and my uncle both rather disapproved of the fact that I had not joined up as my cousins did. So that is why I came back, and, although I dislike nationalism of any form, I think it is rather a dangerous thing, one has roots in a country which are of value. And in many ways I am very glad I stayed here. I do not quite like what happened to England afterwards. I hated the whole system of the English public school and the old-fashioned sort of English superiority of colonialism and everything, I find that most distasteful. Each time I go back to England I find it more and more a foreign country.

MT But you would not have had the opportunity to study composition in Ireland at that stage had you wanted to?

BB Well, of course I did in a way. I think my vagueness about what I learned from Patrick Hadley and Herbert Howells really emphasises the fact that I regard myself more as a self-taught composer; I discovered things myself through my own enthusiasms and trial and error, which suited me because I see quite a number of composers who seem to be dominated by the system that they were taught, which somehow seems to shackle them. It may give them a facility to do things but they are done in a certain way which may not necessarily release that person's individuality. When I became a professional musician I decided I must take a music degree. I was working at the Royal College in order to take the Trinity Mus.B. and as that had been disrupted by the war I decided I must continue with this. I went to John Larchet,[10] Professor of Music at UCD who also taught at the Academy of Music in Dublin, and I had lessons with him for the Mus.B. Larchet was an extremely good technician. I do not think he was a great musician, he was not all that imaginative, but I did hear from other people that Larchet was one of those who had had to work very hard in order to become as distinguished a musician as he was, and he did not find it easy. People like that are often extremely good teachers. Larchet was a marvellous teacher of standard harmony and counterpoint, but I do not think he was a good teacher of composition. The main thing he used to say to me was 'I think you should cut a few bars, it's a bit long'. But he was great at teaching you how to do harmony and counterpoint. A lot of people might disapprove of this attitude to doing harmony and counterpoint, but I believe that any discipline, however distantly related, or even not related, to the thing you have to do finally, any discipline is worthwhile. Just like the discipline of learning Latin or Greek, it frees the mind, and I found the discipline of working at harmony and counterpoint for the degree course extremely good, and Larchet very good at putting you through that. I got my Mus.B. at Trinity the same year as Havelock Nelson[11] (another scientist, a bacteriologist). We both took our Mus.D. at more or less the same time. I took the Mus.D. because several friends of my parents were terribly keen that I should go for the Chair of Music in Trinity,[12] which they knew George Hewson was going to vacate fairly shortly, and in order to qualify for that position it was more or less necessary to have a Doctorate and in those days that meant Mus.D. The Mus.D. exam then was a senior Mus.B. Instead of doing five-part harmony you did eight-part: everything was just a little bit more crossword-puzzley and complicated. I had to work hard on that because I was never very quick and I found it an awful struggle, but it was awfully good for me, I am sure it was. I was quite certain when I took the examination in 1959 that I had failed but, much to my surprise, I passed. So, that was learning with Larchet.

MT   Were there other opportunities for composition lessons?

BB   I had several quite interesting short courses of lessons from Jean Martinon[13] who came over in about 1947 to conduct the orchestra. He was an up and coming young French composer at the time. The Department of Education ran summer schools for which they would engage people to teach composition, conducting and all sorts of things, and so I went along and I had lessons from him. Martinon was a marvellous teacher of conducting and gave quite stimulating lessons in composition. It was very interesting to get another viewpoint. Again, one picked up criticism. He hated Sibelius. I remember trying to convert him but he just regarded it as long pages of padding. But I became very friendly with him and the contact was very useful. Bax[14] and Rawsthorne[15] were doing the same job and I went along to pick up what I could each time and found those contacts very stimulating.

MT   Did you feel at all cut off from the mainstream of music when you came back here? Did you miss all that stimulation?

BB   Well, one replaced it in two ways: the first was gramophone records and you could come across quite a lot of new things on gramophone records. One company produced a lot of records of experimental new music like quartertone music by Hába,[16] and some of the little symphonies of Milhaud, Casella and other Italian composers. I also came across Prokofiev, Poulenc and people like that whom I find a different kind of stimulus. I was very influenced by Prokofiev for some time and it was a shared enthusiasm with a great friend of mine. We used to listen to records avidly, spend all night listening to them and so one partly made up there. There was very little on the radio during the war, though one picked up what one could, but the second way was one organised it oneself. I felt, when I came back, that the place was a desert, and I had to do something about it, and so I used to organise little societies where we would have chamber music concerts and actually play the stuff as best we could. I remember persuading Charles Lynch to include the Berg Sonata[17] at one of his recitals. We tried to produce as much as we could and there was a very nice feeling in those days, there was far less of the attitude that you could not get a thing performed unless you paid people. It is quite extraordinary to think that the first performances of many of my own works were given by my friends, the young professional musicians at the time, who were perfectly happy, so generously, to say they would play my music. I decided that if painters have one-man-shows, why should not a composer put on a one-man-show, and my father very decently paid for a room in the Shelbourne Hotel and these various friends of mine very kindly and very generously performed my *String Trio*, my *Oboe Quintet* (in which I played oboe), my future wife sang some songs with string quartet, and I sang (with flute and string trio) a cycle of songs I had written (to surrealist texts by a friend of mine) called *The Feather of Death*. All the people taking part, most of whom are now quite distinguished senior musicians in Dublin and elsewhere, were only too glad to do that for nothing. It is something that is so generous, I have always felt extremely grateful for people doing that in those days.

I was conducting the chief amateur orchestra in Dublin, the Dublin Orchestral Players, which had been founded in 1939. Their first conductor was Havelock Nelson but he went to

Belfast, where he became accompanist in the BBC, and I took over the orchestra in about 1941 and that was another excitement. First of all, I was able to teach myself conducting, that is really what it came to, and doing so with an amateur orchestra is an extremely good thing to do because you have different kinds of responsibilities. But there was also the opportunity to put on music you were enthusiastic about. The trouble is the limitations of amateur capability, and some of the performances we gave were undoubtedly dire, but I think they made up in enthusiasm for what they may have lost in perfection. Certainly we were often the only people producing public orchestral concerts in Dublin. At that time the Radio Orchestra was shut up in a studio in Henry Street and they came out for one year, gave some concerts in the Mansion House but then decided for some reason to discontinue them, and they went back to their studio. So nobody in Dublin could hear live orchestral music except from the Dublin Orchestral Players. It was a most extraordinary situation that we fulfilled that very important function at one time. I know that the standard of playing was probably absolutely appalling but at least it provided something and I meet people quite often who say they remember the excitement of attending one of my concerts in the early '40s. In fact I was doing my best just fired by enthusiasm to plug holes in what was pretty well a musical desert. Contemporary music came into it as much as possible. There was the Dublin Music Club too in which I was involved, which ran chamber music concerts and recitals, and one tried to put contemporary works into those.

MT   You were involved in a great many things.

BB   Some people attempt to do an awful lot of things and could easily be accused of dabbling and doing none of them perfectly, whereas others just go absolutely bang onto one thing and perfect it. Well I am in the first category. I am a dabbler and probably have never done anything as well as I ought to, but if I had my life again I would do exactly the same because I believe enormously in a broadness of experience. I feel there are far too many uneducated musicians in this world, for instance, who know nothing about anything except music. That means, I think, they are lesser people. The frightfully efficiently-written music, by specialists who have no interest in things outside music, can be quite entertaining in an eighteenth-century way, but it has not got that much personality. And I find that with quite a number of slick composers today who have little imagination. Broadness of outlook led me into painting. I exhibited in the Living Art exhibition three years running, and was loosely attached to a very interesting avant-garde movement in Dublin, the White Stag Group. I say loosely because I was mixed up in music and many other things at the same time, but I exhibited with them.

MT Did you have sympathies with avant-garde composers as well as artists?

BB Schoenberg and co. were the avant-garde then, so was Walton. He is so much old hat now I cannot believe that he was. I heard the second performance of the First Symphony[18] and I also remember being overwhelmed by *Belshazzar's Feast*[19] and we all knew *Façade*.[20] Of course people like Milhaud were in their way quite avant-garde too, those short symphonies and his bitonal and polytonal compositions. I experimented with those ideas – with bitonality – but not until a little later. The rather thick texture of the early Berg romantic music such as the Op. 2 songs[21] (which I sang) was beginning to creep into my work.

MT Did you ever feel any desire to go to Vienna to study?

BB It never occurred to me for some reason, but I wonder how far I thought myself as a future composer or a future musician. I am not absolutely certain. I just felt a desire to write, and wrote. It gradually became more important in my life and at the time that I was painting, for instance, I suddenly stopped and thought 'in order to paint well, and I know I am not painting well, I will have to devote more time to it, that will mean that I have got to make a decision, am I going to paint or write music', and I decided I must perfect my writing of music. And so I think that I really began to become a composer about 1943/44. Before that, I regarded myself as trying out all sorts of possible channels and finally deciding on composition. At a slightly later stage, I think it must have been about 1947, I remember Hubert Clifford was over taking the conducting class that Martinon gave. He used to be the conductor and composer for the Rank Organisation, and I always remember him taking me aside and saying 'Brian, you will have to decide whether you want to conduct or compose, you cannot do both.

In fact when I look around the only person I know who has made a success of both conducting and composing is myself.' And I think the number of people who have heard of poor Hubert Clifford must be rather small. So this whole idea of trying to narrow down was a slow process. I matured really very late, I am well aware of that.

MT   When you came back to Ireland, on the outbreak of war, did you suddenly find yourself in the vanguard?

BB   Not for a bit. I think the first time that I produced a shocking piece of music, which everybody said was dreadful, because it was too modern, was with my tongue in my cheek. One of the first professional jobs as a composer I got was writing theatre music for a series of productions at the Olympia Theatre. I wrote music to a satirical play which I then produced as a satirical suite after I had heard Mosolov's[22] *Iron Foundry* on a record. I remember talking about this with some of my friends and saying how easy it is to write this sort of thing, and so I wrote a bit of foundry music which I called *The Hammond Lane Serenade* (Hammond Lane was a big iron foundry in Dublin which was extant in those days). I performed this with the Dublin Orchestral Players and that created a great furore, some people thought it was great fun, others were disgusted and furious. The first work that stamped me as a dangerous avant-garde was my first String Quartet. Previous to that I had written the Five Joyce Songs, and at that stage I was conscious of being fairly avant-garde because I simplified my technique on purpose for the Joyce Songs, having noticed how Joyce's lyrics are so enormously simple and straightforward compared with his prose. I still like those songs, I think they are well written; they are not avant-garde in any violent sense at all, certainly not today. But the string quartet was definitely a dangerous modern noise, and I also wrote a work which Martinon conducted which I gave an Irish title *Magh Sleacht* bringing out my intense interest in the ceremonies which went on in Megalithic Ireland around the stone circles, an interest I shared with Arnold Bax. Seóirse Bodley tells me that he got up and walked out when it was performed because it was too modern for his ears, then later Seóirse was writing music that went right beyond my comprehension. Another contemporary orchestral work, *In Memoriam Mahatma Gandhi*, now sounds not terribly avant-garde, but for the time it was fairly modern.

MT   How well did you know Bax?

BB   I first met him in connection with the Summer School and then we became very friendly, and he was a very close friend of Aloys Fleischmann,[23] in fact he was to have dined in our house the night he died. Whenever he came over we would always meet and have a meal, and we would go for a drive in the country, generally to visit some Megalithic tombs. But I cannot say I knew him intimately.

MT   Did you find this a strange experience because you must have known from your time in London and Cambridge that this was not really avant-garde, and yet here you were regarded as something of an *enfant terrible*.

BB   I think there are several pressures on a composer, which are not necessarily comfortable or uncomfortable, of which one has to be terribly careful. One of them is a certain sneaking desire for notoriety that I think an awful lot of composers fall victim to. One of the ways of doing that is to make a shocking kind of noise, to do something strange, which is very close to being frightfully original, and I think this can be an extremely dangerous thing. One enjoys the notoriety of being regarded as dangerously avant-garde but that can be very dangerous because then you may think entirely about being avant-garde or making highly original noises to the detriment of your true creative personality. That is something that has distorted the creativity of a great many creative artist: painters, composers and many others, who cannot resist the idea of trying to be frightfully original, and this becomes an end in itself. One can become so entirely bound up in the fascination of doing a certain technical thing, such as writing in a very avant-garde technique, that you forget about the real point of creativity, and tie your personality in knots. This whole business about originality or being avant-garde comes down to something which has crystallised in my mind over a very long period, and that is honesty of purpose. The most valuable thing in all creativity is that, no matter what the pressures may be, you must be yourself, but then you have got to know yourself to know that the part of yourself which you think is yourself is the honest, true one.

    That was illustrated by another type of influence here which was very strong. During the forties composers in this country were split into two rival camps. There were those who felt that we are Irish, that we must write Irish music and make use of the wonderful traditional melodies, whereas the other side (which included Fred May,[24] myself, and Aloys Fleischmann who came over to our side) felt that creative artists must be sensitive people who can absorb influences from their surroundings. If you live in this country and are of this country, those influences soak into your bones and therefore we felt our job was to express ourselves in an internationally understood language, in fact the language of contemporary European music. What lay behind the language would automatically be coloured by the fact that you were Irish and lived here, without having to try and be Irish. The other side were producing what I call the plastic shamrock, the sort of thing that exported extremely well to America and in fact, I think, has done the image of serious music in this country a lot of damage. They were following the Irish folksong tradition. Stanford started it by marrying so-called Irish folksong, which had already been a good deal altered and tidied up, to Brahmsian or teutonic harmony. It was carried on by Larchet, who was adept at it, and handed on to Ó Gallchobháir,[25] Tommy Kelly[26] and Redmond Friel.[27] Freddie May and I avoided that like the plague, but the funny thing is that when I wrote my second String Quartet one of these ardent Gaelic types came up to me and said he was so glad that I had taken his advice and used a particular Irish tune, and, of course, I had never heard the thing, it just came out.

MT   What advantages did returning to Ireland have for you as a composer?

BB   The student I shared a flat with when I was at the Royal College was an enormously prolific composer. He was also a tremendous disciplinarian: he set himself the task of writing a song a day for a year, which he did. He had also written five symphonies. He was three years older than me and had been a previous organ scholar at Clare College. He was doing the fourth year of the Mus.B. in my first year at Cambridge when I met him. He had written all this music but never had a note of it performed. You get very discouraged if you are writing music without a performance; I might have turned to painting or something else. This is only something one realises later, and that is many English composers in his position (and probably, had I stayed in England, in my position) would never have got anywhere at all. There was a distinct advantage to being the big fish in the little pond. But at least when we got to the fifties we reached a stage where the radio organisation would actually perform any reasonably competent piece by an Irish composer. That was one of the side advantages of the slightly chauvinistic business that the radio here was only too keen to fly an Irish flag. The number of composers active in the forties in this country you could count on the fingers of your hands. It has increased enormously since because things have developed so much, but one had a chance here. The reason that I wrote two string quartets was partly because I like writing quartets more than anything, I think it is the finest of all musical mediums, but the other reason was that quartets here wanted them; I wrote so many part-songs because the RTÉ singers were always wanting Irish part-songs; and the radio wanted orchestral works. So there was always a performance coming up. Admittedly, one did not often get many more after the first one, although my first String Quartet was being played a lot. It is a great encouragement to feel that your music is wanted, and I think one needs encouragement. It is not a paying concern but one of the best recompenses is to feel that you are giving some pleasure to somebody else, but mainly, that it is appreciated.

MT   You have gone from what might be described as the angry young man of Irish music to being the grand old man. Do you think that that had any implications for your music, that transition? Do you think you have mellowed, become part of the musical establishment? And do you think it is more stimulating or liberating for a creative artist to be working from the outside rather than from the inside of the establishment?

BB   I have become a lot more tolerant; or have I? I am aware of the fact that the very avant-garde things happening at the moment have moved outside my way of thinking and I respect that they can have perfect validity. The experience of a long time at it lets you see certain things in perspective. I have noticed how easily, what you might call an avant-garde trick, can become the empty cliché of the next generation. I am impatient with the idea that the past values have no relevance to today,

whereas I believe that there is a great deal of room for re-affir-
mation of permanent values in the context of today. It is such
a complex business, composition. Some people might regard it
as part of the entertainment business; I am very much
concerned with things like preservation of the earth and
ecology, and want to be able to say this in a language which
effects the senses directly. I am still, I suppose, romantic
enough to be much more interested in music which moves me
emotionally than music which fascinates me purely intellectu-
ally, although the fact that my blank spot is nineteenth-century
Italian opera shows that I am not purely of that kind. I am not
satisfied with a bit of music with an oom-pah bass. In fact I like
an intellectual content. That is why I am so fond of Brahms
because he has the emotional warmth and this absolutely fascinating intellectual construction throughout; the logic of its
construction.

MT   You are talking about two different areas of response there
      presumably.

BB   Yes, I think the two areas of response come together. I find
      with much contemporary music today that I can say 'yes, that
      is very interesting and I find that a fascinating noise', but it
      does not touch me emotionally at all, and therefore it is not
      really for me. But any opinion about the arts from anybody,
      however distinguished, tells you more about that person than
      it does about the arts, and all the opinions that I may be
      quoting now and ideas about music really tell you more about
      me and my preferences than anything that explains anything in
      music.

MT   Do you think the change in your position has had an effect on
      your creative writing?

BB   I find it impossible to assess my creative writing at the present
      time. Sometimes when I hear some of the better earlier works
      that I wrote, I feel, my goodness, I could not do that now. I
      somehow think I wrote my best music years ago and I have
      really just been paddling along ever since. I am terribly anxious
      about anything I write.

MT   You do not feel that your grand-old-man status inhibits you in
      any way from doing something you might want to do
      musically?

BB   I suppose there is a slight fear; there is the awful fear that at this stage, having some kind of reputation, more is expected of you than possibly may be delivered by the work I have produced. I would have gone in with tremendous confidence if I had written a new work in 1950, feeling I was absolutely confident this is the right thing, and if they do not like it, it is their fault. Whereas now I have the awful terror that, if they do not like it, it might well be my fault.

MT But that would not lead you to play safe would it?

BB No, it would not.

MT Seóirse Bodley[28] writes in *Grove* that your style of composition has remained essentially unchanged throughout your creative career. Is that true?

BB No, I think it is not really true. There are thumbprints of mine which have gone the whole way through, but there have been certain definite directions in which I have moved from one time to another. For instance, in my *String Trio* of 1943, which I would regard as the first work in which I found some kind of an individual voice, quite intuitively, I hit on the idea of a scale of alternate tones and semitones. It was not until twelve years after that I discovered that Messiaen had also used it. The first Quartet is all built on that kind of scale too. I soon learnt that, just like the whole-tone scale as manipulated by Debussy, you cannot stick to it because it only has three transpositions and leads to diminished sevenths logically, which somehow have an outworn feeling. Then in the fifties I discovered the new sound of fourteenth-century music, particularly Guillaume de Machaut, and that absolutely fascinated me. *Mors et Vita*, a large choral work for wind instruments, choir and soloists, is very much influenced by the medieval thing, so was my second Quartet.

MT Would these be specific techniques, or just the sound?

BB No, just the sound, a first inversion minor chord slipping down a semitone, which you get in Machaut, and a Phrygian mode feeling where you have a flattened supertonic, but mostly bare fourths, avoidance of the rather more romantic sweet intervals of thirds and sixths, concentrating on fourths and sevenths and bare octaves. I had long been interested in counterpoint, and the crossword puzzle-type harmony and counterpoint that one did was enormously valuable as a training in manipulating notes. but I really got a feeling for counterpoint from singing it in the Cambridge Madrigal Society under Boris Ord. Throughout those three years singing great masses of sixteenth-century polyphony was a marvellous thing and I learnt far more from singing sixteenth-century music than from studying it in classes.

MT Do you think then Bodley was specifically referring to surface phenomena?

BB I would say so, yes, because to compare my early Joyce songs with any of the string quartets or *In Memoriam Mahatma Gandhi*, they are, to me, totally different works. Then *Mors et Vita* and the first movement particularly of the second String Quartet, display the sort of mediaeval things which are quite different from anything which occurs in the *Violin Concerto* for instance. Also in the fifties, I think it came from an enthusiasm for Stravinsky and Bartók (particularly the Romanian and Bulgarian rhythms), is experimenting with uneven rhythms. The first example is in the last movement of my second String Quartet. I developed that further in the *Quintet for Flute, Harp and String Trio*, it comes into the last movement of the *Symphonic Inscapes*, and I use it again in this new work I have just written, *Masai Mara*. I find this idea of a group of three happening in a string of groups of two enormously exciting, giving a sort of spring-board effect, it is like that extra hop before you take a dive off a spring-board, and it hurls the rhythm forward. One of the things that I find most stimulating is the rhythmic excitement of music and that is why an awful lot of contemporary music bores me stiff, because it just does not move at all. I know you can argue that a lot of these very complex pieces of apparently static music have a rhythmic impulse behind them of great complexity, but I am thinking of the pure sensuous impact of rhythm in music. I find that a terribly important thing, rather like the old accusation that modern music has no decent tune. I remember hearing Prokofiev playing his third Piano Concerto in the Queen's Hall in London before the war and that was terribly exciting. Now that was a pretty modern sound in those days. I thought it was a nasty sound and that there were no tunes in it. How I thought that it is hard to imagine.

MT You have been very frank about your own prejudices and preferences. How difficult do you find it in your various activities, performing, lecturing, broadcasting, administration, the Arts Council, PRS,[29] to respond to something towards which you are not particularly sympathetic?

BB It has always been a problem. I think it is akin to adjudicating. I developed the rather curious craft of adjudicating which was one of my main ways of making a living before I became an academic. In adjudicating I think one has to train oneself to do it as a job. I very seldom enjoy a piece of music when I am adjudicating because I have trained myself to listen in a way which I disapprove of, and that is looking for the faults as well as the good points. As Professor I found it extremely difficult judging people's exercises for degrees. If somebody wrote in a style which I do not particularly like I think I tend to lean over backwards a bit there, but generally the one thing I am pretty adamant about is that a really good firm technique in handling the material is essential for all artists. It is perfectly possible if somebody brings me an extremely advanced type of post-Webern composition, which I do not particularly like, to see that this is well done.

MT When you come to a new composition do you find the fact that you are personally acquainted with so many other composers inhibits you from giving a completely frank assessment? Would you actually say that you did not like it and leave it at that?

BB I think the first answer is yes, one does feel inhibited because you know the composer, one tends to have a prejudice built in before even looking at the work. But the other thing in answering is that I am terribly slow to commit myself that this is good or this is bad. I am always conscious of the failure of human nature in criticism, and this fact which I realise more and more is true, that is any critical opinion tells you more about the critic than it does about the work of art. I have been anxious all my life because I think I have got further in many ways than I deserve to have done. I have always been conscious of the lack of facility. I would argue now that a certain lack of facility is probably a good thing because it makes you struggle, and I believe the struggle of writing something tends to bring out the best, a sort of challenge. Writing the more complex contrapuntal sections of some of the earlier works was a very big struggle. I would work for a long time, maybe days on one or two bars and then go away and garden, or fish, and then the whole thing would solve itself in my mind without my knowing it. When I came to be Professor of Music at Trinity College, completely fresh from a life as a general musician, conducting, lecturing, composing, organising music, it may have been an advantage because I brought a fresh view of the whole thing, but I was conscious of the fact that in many ways I was an amateur Professor. All my colleagues had been in academic life all the time; I think it restricted them.

MT   What about music criticism? There you have the two areas: that one is trying to encourage on the one hand, and on the other to offer an honest appraisal.

BB   I think that if the newspaper critics had built up a reputation as people who really had a very good knowledge of music (and that does mean somebody who has been through the mill himself and knows what it is like to conduct an orchestra or rehearse a choir) that is the sort of criticism I would take notice of.

MT   How far do you think the argument could be advanced that what the public needs now with works that are unfamiliar is unequivocally good performance?

BB   I know to my cost what appalling performances some of my works have had, but I do not think the right way to try to get a better one is to write in a newspaper, for a non-musical public, that this was awful. The way to get better performances is by encouragement from somebody who knows the job better, and I have several times taken it upon myself to go privately to my colleagues, some of them very senior colleagues, and point out things which I think would help to get a better performance. It needs great tact and a certain amount of courage. People have done the same to me, people who I admire. Aloys Fleischmann, for instance, I found is the only person whose criticism of my composition has been really of value, he is able to look at a thing and somehow he has an instinct of knowing little things that are not quite right as they should be, and he will always say so. I respect his judgement because he knows his job.

MT   But do you think there is enough of that?

BB   Not as much as there should be. I think people are afraid to. But I think performers as well as creative artists are very sensitive people. One has to be awfully careful not just to slap them in the face.

MT   Do you think economic considerations have been used as an excuse for not rehearsing pieces properly?

BB   Oh yes. I felt for a long time that one of the great snags of the development of music in our time has been the much greater facility of sight-reading. Now that may sound an absolutely mad thing to say but it is a paradox like many of these strange things, the result is now that you get a certain number of rehearsals, and, since musicians are such good sight-readers, they play all the notes probably more or less right and they sing all the notes more or less right, but they never actually get into the bones of the piece. That was one of the things that I went for when I formed the Dowland Consort. We would never perform a work in public in any large concert until we had had it in our repertoire for at least a year. You have got to know what happens not only around the next page but right through the whole work and as you are performing the work you have got to feel how it fits into the whole thing. You must have an intimate feeling in vocal music for the meaning of the words you are singing. There was an interesting performance done technically quite well recently of the Agnus Dei from the four-part *Mass* of Byrd, and it sounded awfully nice, but one realises that I do not think any of those singers was thinking beyond making a nice sound here, or getting a little louder there. They never really got right inside the extraordinary mystical quality of that music, the result is that it came out rather like an exercise, but it was hard to fault technically.

MT   One of the things that lay behind that question is the future of composition for large orchestra where it seems to me that if you are going to play a big piece for orchestra the likelihood of repetition is small, and so one should be uneconomic and spend the necessary time to have the piece performed decently.

BB   Naturally it is a thing I have thought about but I do not know if I have ever faced up to it in any practical way. The first thing is a composer wants to hear his work done at almost at any cost and the opportunity has been handed out here. If somebody wants to do a work of mine I will write it, because you know you are getting the performance, it is what you really want. And I suppose we have got used to having not very good performances.

MT   It made me wonder, looking at statistics for performances, whether the fact that we have so many first performances and so few second and subsequent ones is somehow conditioned by the fact that we do not have a public beating on the door demanding to hear a piece again, simply because they were so taken with the first performance

BB　There is this curious feeling amongst promoters that, if you put in a work by a contemporary Irish composer, you will not fill the hall. I think they are wrong. I think you can slip the work in amongst other things. That is the way I would tackle it and that is what used to happen with the Gaiety Proms in the old days. Practically every concert had some shortish work by an Irish composer slipped in somewhere, and I think that was a good thing. But it is the same the world over; the number of people who want to hear a work by a contemporary composer as compared to the number of people who want to hear Tchaikovsky's Piano Concerto again is small. During the 1950s the broadcasting organisation here was the best encouragement that any composer could wish for. They had a professional string quartet, a professional chamber choir, and a professional orchestra, all of whom were crying out for works to perform, and it was absolutely marvellous that at least you got your work performed. Admittedly it was not repeated that often, but that did not happen anywhere. That was a marvellous incentive and that is why so many string quartets have been written by Irish composers, so much unaccompanied vocal music and so on. But things are not so good now at the moment. I think I am lucky in a way because I managed to make a name for myself during the time when things were going well, so that certain of my works do get performed more now than some other people.

MT　Denis Donoghue said you tend to drop your critical sights when you come across something labelled made in Ireland.

BB　I may well have done at the time, I do not think so now. I am definitely not a nationalist in the sense of fighting for my country, or everything Irish is better, it is not that at all, but I was concerned with trying to persuade other people that there were a lot of things in Ireland that were far better than they knew about. That explains why I was always very keen to try and push Irish composition. It is really to redress the balance because for so long there was this patronising attitude that

1. *Brian Boydell, school portrait, c.1926*

2. Boydell in 1936

6. Caricature of Boydell in the
Evening Herald *announcing a series*
of concerts, 10 November 1945

4. *Boydell in 1955 (Photo: Andrew Skilling)*

5. 'Surrealoid' drawing, c. 1943

6. 'Surrealoid' drawing, c. 1943

7. Boydell, c. 1950

8. *Brian Boydell with Tibor Paul and Igor Stravinsky, 1963*

9. 1993 (Photo: Axel Klein)

nothing good could come out of this country, and indeed that was the kind of image that was being portrayed in America with what I refer to as the plastic shamrock. And so it was really a feeling that we did produce rather better things here than we were credited for and therefore that made me appear to be a little bit more pro-Irish than I actually was underneath.

MT   Much of your music in recent years has been commissioned. Do you personally find you need this direct motivation to compose?

BB   I enjoy it. I like a challenge. I think I am getting lazier now and I do not stir my stumps to do something if there is no goal to go for. It is rather different from what I used to be long ago; I think I am just getting lazy. I like a goal to aim for and a commission provides that goal very conveniently. It makes me get down to work and do it. I like even having a deadline to meet, it is all part of the challenge. So I have enjoyed commissions in that way. It is some time since I have written a work which was not actually commissioned, although the last quartet was not.

MT   You are in a somewhat enviable position in that it is possible for you to try and marry together a commissioner's needs and what you feel you would like to write. A younger composer would not have the clout to be able to get the commissioner to commission the piece that he wanted to write. Are you worried that one of the unexpected by-products of the Arts Council's commission scheme could be that composers are not really writing what they want to write anymore, but are waiting until somebody asks them to write something.

BB   I remember having a long chat with Samuel Barber when he was in Dublin and he said he only really got down to writing music when he was bored. If you want to be cynical you would say a lot of his music may sound like that, but I know what he means exactly because I think I was in the same situation some time in the forties. I can just get an inkling of it: you know that you are searching for something you want to do, what you are doing at the moment is not fully satisfying, you want something to do, I would love to write a so-and-so, and off you go. It was a long time before I was ever commissioned to write anything.

MT   That is probably a good thing though.

BB I think so, because if I had no burning desire to write music I would not have gone on with it because you got very little back in those days.

MT When you were talking to Charles Acton in 1970[30] you mentioned that when you went to Trinity you anticipated that it would mean a cessation of composing for about ten years.

BB I thought it would, but it did not turn out that way.

MT Do you find you can make a deliberate decision like that, not to compose for a certain period of time?

BB Oh no, it was not a decision, it was facing a fact. During my time at Trinity I never really wrote anything more than perhaps just a very short little thing at all during the academic year, it was always after the year ended. I did occasionally get some work done at the Christmas break, but I need an uninterrupted period where nothing else like meetings of the Arts Council comes in, and I can just think about this and then meditate in the garden or whatever may be handy at the time. I thought it would have to be because having made the rather difficult decision to take on that job when I was offered it, I was determined to make the best of it. Working towards setting up a proper teaching School of Music, which I eventually did, was a struggle against academics who just could not believe that music was an academic subject at all. That needed an awful lot of thought and energy, and also, if you like, learning the job, finding out what was going on and creating a good university situation.

MT What is your opinion of the standard of teaching and the way music is taught in Ireland?

BB There are two aspects. One of the things that I set out to do was to try and get rid of what I think is an appalling attitude to the teaching of the fundamental theoretical aspects of music, the old Kitson[31] approach where you learn harmony as a series of dots on paper and are never trained to use your ear. You learn a series of rules which you must not break, without ever learning why. That was perpetuated here because, being a rather small country, practically everyone was so-and-so's pupil, and the next generation were all the pupils of that one. So things got stuck in the old Kitson tradition. Joe Groocock[32] and I, when I was developing the School of Music in Trinity, were determined to see if we could do something about this and change the direction of teaching, so that it became related to real music. We introduced the idea that no exercise is just corrected on a blackboard or on paper but it is played or sung. And you do not say 'there are consecutive fifths, it is wrong', but you stop, if there are consecutive fifths or something like that in an exercise done by a student, and you either play it, or better still they all sing it, and you say 'is there anything wrong there? Does that sound a bit odd?' In fact to bring the ear in as judge and to relate the whole business of 'correct' harmony and counterpoint, to real musical sound. I think we succeeded in changing things in that way. But it is a very wide-ranging question because the teaching of harmony and counterpoint is only one aspect of teaching. My own feeling about the teaching of any subject as a whole is that the prime object is to instil enthusiasm in the student, and if you can do that the rest almost follows. That is the most important thing: to make the students love the subject and enjoy learning about it. History of music used to be taught as a series of written statements connected to music which was never heard, but history must be connected with the sound, it must be made interesting.

MT What about instrumental teaching?

BB I do think the intense competitiveness is a great pity – I do not know how one can get around it all – but this idea that you are no good unless you have won a *premier prix* or the Leeds Piano Competition or the Dublin one, this whole idea I found distasteful and terribly hard on those people who do not win, who are probably extremely good. When I started out earning my living teaching singing I would never let my students get involved in this business of the competitive musical festival idea unless they wished to on their own, but the first thing I would insist on is that you must learn the very difficult technique of using the voice. In fact I was the only person in Dublin teaching voice production intensively at that time, stressing the idea that you must not actually go and sing in public until you have learnt how to play the instrument so to speak. I used to say that as far as singing teaching is concerned that if you happened to be born with a nice voice it is rather like happening to have parents rich enough to give you a present of a Steinway grand when you are a young pianist. You have got to learn how to play the thing before you can make any music, and people assume that if you happen to be able to make a nice noise with your voice by some kind of natural situation, as happens from time to time, all you have got to do is sing in your bath a little and the next thing you are on the stage in La Scala. You must have complete command of the technique and then you are free enough to be able to say what you want to.

MT   You have often spoken about your strong belief in broadness of experience, do you feel that musical composition fails to allow you a complete outlet for self-expression? Is that why you wanted to paint?

BB   I would not have thought of it in those terms. I have always wanted to do a lot of things and I have consciously blocked out interests in certain things which I thought would take too much energy away from things one might hope to cover. Fishing was enough, and gardening – they are both contemplative things – I actually find I do a great deal of work while I am doing those, but the thing at the moment that is fascinating me more than anything is historical musicology. At the moment I have just finished one paper and want to complete a book studying the music for the Rotunda Hospital in the second half of the eighteenth century, showing all the changes in taste and so on. I want to learn more about the social life and politics of the eighteenth century. During periods of my life I have gone off composition and gone onto something else, and I see myself in a slightly 'off' position now. I cannot think just at the moment of anything that is exciting me, or a new idea that I want to say at the moment having just completed *Masai Mara,* apart from wanting to write some more vocal music to words which I make up myself.

MT   Can we talk a little about the new piece, *Masai Mara?*

BB   The new piece really comes from an expression of something which has been in my mind for a very long time but it was brought to the surface by visiting the great game parks of Kenya, where I had an extraordinary feeling of experiencing what the earth was like before human beings came along and started spoiling it. One felt that one was in these game parks as a guest of the animals who have been there for thousands of years, and there was something really primeval about it and the sounds one heard. There was a very remarkable bird that one heard very often, with an extraordinary kind of call. It started just on one note going slowly, getting faster and faster and then a little fall at the end, and that I found a unique kind of sound. One of the loveliest records that I have in my library of gramophone records is a recording made on one of the north Canadian lakes during a late summer evening where the loons, as they call them there, we call them Great Northern Divers, start calling to each other across the lake in the evening with the echoes coming back from the trees. I am very much concerned about ecology and people ruining the environment, and pollution of one kind or another, far more dangerous than any atomic bomb at the moment. These ideas all came together and I wanted to express them in some way, and the idea of this orchestral piece brings those points to the fore. The title of the work gave me some trouble. At first, I thought I was going to call it *Greenpeace*, but then I realised that has political overtones, so that did not suit me at all. Then I started thinking of those little phrases that can be interpreted in two ways, like *Earth cries*, but I thought that too gimmicky. Finally I decided to give it the name of the biggest game park in Kenya *Masai Mara* which is just a nice sounding name. It is a loose title just referring to impressions which came to my head in that place. Fundamentally the idea that I wanted to get across was a feeling of a primeval kind of world with threatening rumbles in the background, and a slight feeling of pain at the disturbance. Partly for a sense of musical, and also dramatic contrast, there is a nasty disruptive section in the middle before a return to the first idea now transformed into a type of nirvana, with an idea of hope, that in the end natural forces may win through. One once more gets a completely peaceful or natural situation. At least it is not in the form of anything practical – it is more some kind of a dream. The form is a slow atmospheric section, a middle part which is disturbing and prickly with the kind of uneven rhythms that I rather like, and then a return to the slow material of the beginning, only this time transformed into some kind of expression of eternal peacefulness and nirvana. One of the problems straight away was that I wanted to use some of these birdcalls as fundamental material which could give rise to many other things, and to find an orchestral instrument that made the right noise. A curious thing, there is no orchestral instrument with the formants that sound the vowel oo except the horn. But the horn has the wrong kind of attack being a lip attack. There are instruments that are not used in the orchestra, for instance, ideally, the ocarina, and to some extent, a swanee whistle too. But it is no use writing for an ocarina because you will never get the piece performed as they never find a player. After a lot of experiment, I hit on the idea of using a tenor recorder, if possible, a renaissance model; not a baroque one because the renaissance tenor recorder is just a little bit nearer to the quality I want. And so I scored using a renaissance tenor recorder and had the cooperation of a great friend of mine who is a very good recorder player in working out the possibilities. One of the snags with the recorder is to play it in tune, but I instruct the player not to try to play in tune, and I have a special notation for bending the pitch and pushing a note definitely sharp so that it stands on a different plane from the other things that are going on around it. The bird remains free, if you like, without being bound to the other things around it. One of the things about the cry of the loon is it has an extraordinary way of jumping up as though it is breaking into a series of harmonics, only the harmonics are in fourths. A lot of the ideas come from these birdcalls; the thematic material becomes imbued with my falling minor third. Then the middle section uses uneven rhythms, seven-eight for example. There are places where I do not actually quote from certain earlier works but use material that occurs most notably in both the first and second string quartets, because in a way they just suited the kind of feeling that I wanted to get into the music; I do not just quote them, but develop them in a slightly different direction. Anybody who did happen to know the quartets would say I had just pinched it from there. I did not just pinch it from there and I thought a lot about whether is it cheating to use things you have written before. But I am not using them in the same way as I had before, and also they are slightly altered and in a totally different context. And I found this perfectly legitimate.

MT   How would you characterise the harmonic language of the piece?

BB   The opening slowly builds up a series of very wide chords in harmonics on the strings, great big chords that spread right through the range mostly built of sevenths and fourths. These chords are not built up from any kind of theoretical reasoning – they are just collections of notes that I like the sound of. Those sorts of interval are used later when the disturbing things start to impinge on the opening. A figure emerges which descends very quickly a major seventh and then jumps up a sixth to the note a minor third below the first one, that is carried down right through the orchestra. In one sense this work is a risk, and I wonder whether I shall have succeeded in creating a curiously static kind of magic. It is a work that depends on almost entirely on atmosphere, and whether one has hit it off or not is a thing I just have to wait and see.

MT   How would you regard the piece in relation to other works you have written recently?

BB   Recently I have been writing rather light-hearted, humorous, even funny music. I have rather had that feeling that many contemporary artists take themselves so desperately seriously. And I think in the end it becomes a little bit boring always to be frightfully serious, and if the creative artist has any duty to humanity one of his duties is quite honestly, to entertain and not always be concerned with telling people about his awful troubles. So I believe there is plenty of room for funny, entertaining music – and I rather enjoy doing it. It just happens that quite a number of the things I have been doing recently have had rather a tongue-in-cheek kind of atmosphere to them. This is the first serious work I have written for some time now and it is a work that had been bubbling away in the back of my mind for a long time when the trigger came in the form of a commission from RTÉ to write an orchestral work.

APPENDICES

I

Compositions by Brian Boydell
Compiled by HAZEL FARRELL

ORCHESTRAL WORKS

Title	Date	Instrumentation	Duration	Additional Information	First Performance
Pregaria a la Verge del Remei, op.14	1941 rev.1945	Str orch	19'	Fantasia on an old Catalan chant Ded: Ralph and Kira Cusack	1942: RIAM, Dublin: DSO, Terry O'Connor (cond.)
The Strings are False, op.16	1942	Orch: 1010/0110/timp/pf/str	5'	Overture to the play by Paul Vincent Carroll Com: Sheila Richards and Michael Walsh	1942: Olympia Theatre Dublin: Theatre Orchestra, Brian Boydell (cond.)
Laish, op.17	1942	Orch: 3222/2231/timp. perc/hp/str	8'	Tone poem	8/6/1943: Metropolitan Hall, Dublin: DOP; Havelock Nelson (cond.)
Satirical Suite, op.18a	1942	Orch: 3222/2231/timp. perc/str.	15' 5 movts	Adapted from the House of Cards, op.18	23/5/1944: Metropolitan Hall, Dublin: DOP, Brian Boydell (cond.)
Symphony for Strings, op.26	1945 rev.1946	Str orch	20' 3 movts	Ded: Mary and Cormac Boydell	30/10/1945: Abbey Lecture Hall, Dublin: DOP, Brian Boydell (cond.)
Magh Sleacht, op.29 Subtitled: The Plain of Prostrations	1947	Orch: 3332/4331/timp. 2perc/pf/str	20' 3 movts		5/9/1947: RÉ: RÉSO, Jean Martinon (cond.)
In memoriam Mahatma Gandhi, op.30	1948	Orch: 2222/4230/perc/str	12'	Ded: Mahatma Gandhi	20/7/1948: Phoenix Hall, Dublin: RÉSO, Brian Boydell (cond.)
Ballet Suite: The Buried Moon, op.32a	1949	Orch: 22(ca)22/2230/timp. perc/str	14' 3 movts		25/2/1950: Whitworth Hall, Drogheda: DOP, Brian Boydell (cond.)
The Wooing of Etain, Suite No.1, op.37a	1954	Orch: 2222/2230/3perc/hp/str	15' 5 movts	Ded: DOP	20/11/1954: Carlow Town Hall: DOP, Brian Boydell (cond.)

Title	Date	Instrumentation	Duration	Additional Information	First Performance
The Wooing of Etain, Suite No.2, op.37b	1954	Orch: 2(pic)2(ca)22/4331/ timp. 3perc/cel.hp/str	14' 4 movts	Ded: Milan Horvat and the Dublin 'Prom' audiences	31/10/1954: Gaiety Theatre, Dublin: RÉSO Milan Horvat (cond.)
Megalithic Ritual Dances, op.39	1956	Orch: 2222/4331/3perc/hp/str	17' 1 movt	Com: RÉ Rec: Decca DL9843 RÉSO, Milan Horvat (cond.)	12/2/1956: Gaiety Theatre, Dublin: RÉSO Milan Horvat (cond.)
Meditation and Fugue, op.40	1956 rev. 1957	Orch: 2222/4231/2perc/str	15' 2 linked movts	Ded: Aloys Fleischmann	20/1/1975: Gaiety Theatre, Dublin: RÉSO, Milan Horvat (cond.)
Ceol Cas Corach, op.46	1958	Orch: 2222/4331/perc/str	10' 1 movt	Ded: Lady Dorothy Mayer	18/1/1959: Gaiety Theatre, Dublin: RÉSO, Maurice Miles (cond.)
Shielmartin Suite, op.47	1958–1959	Orch: 2222/4230/perc/hp/str (also arr. for small orch)	13' 4 movts	Ded: Gráinne Yeats Com: BBC for Festival of Light Music 1960	1/6/1960: Festival Hall, London: BBCCO, Vilm Tausky (cond.)
Symphonic Inscapes, op.64	1968	Orch: 2222(cbn)/4231/ per/hp./cel/pf/str	22' 3 movts	Ded: Patrick Carey Rec: NIRC NIR011, RTÉSO, Albert Rosen (cond.)	26/1/1969: Gaiety Theatre, Dublin: RTÉSO, Albert Rosen (cond.)
Jubilee Music, op.73	1976	Orch: 2222(cbn)/4230/ timp.3perc/cel.hp/str	13'	Ded: RTÉSO Com: RTÉ for the 50th anniversary of Irish broadcasting	3/10/1976: Gaiety Theatre, Dublin: RTÉSO, Albert Rosen (cond.)
Partita Concertante, op.75	1978	Orch: Vn/fl.hp/2222/2000/ perc/str	20'	Adapted from Five Mosaics, op.69 and Impetuous Impromptu, op.75a	2/2/1983: National Concert Hall, Dublin: RTÉSO, Thérèse Timoney, Denise Kelly (hp) John Hopkins (cond)
A Wild Dance for Ceol Chumann na nÓg, op.78	1982	Orch: 2222/4331/timp. 3perc.hp/str	6'	Com: Ceol Chumann na nÓg	11/1/1983: National Concert Hall, Dublin: RTÉSO, John Hughes (cond.)

Title	Date	Instrumentation	Duration	Additional Information	First Performance
Masai Mara, op.87	1988	Orch: 2323/tr.rec/4230/ timp.3perc/hp.str	12'	Com: RTÉ	30/6/1989: National Concert Hall, Dublin: RTÉSO, Kasper de Roo (cond.)
VOICES AND ORCHESTRA					
Hearing of Harvests, op.13	1940	Bar-solo/Orch: 2222/ 4231/timp/str SATB chorus	2.5'	Ded: Charles Acton Text: W.H. Auden	
Five Joyce Songs, op.28a	1946 rev. 1948	Bar-solo/Orch: 1121/0000/str	15'	Text: James Joyce See also op.26 (1946)	1948: Phoenix Hall, Dublin: RÉSO Frederick Fuller (Bar), Brian Boydell (cond.)
The Deer's Cry, op.43	1957	Bar-solo/Orch: 0222/0220	11'	Text: Trans. from Old Irish by Thomas Kinsella	10/11/1957: The Pocket Theatre, Dublin: DOP, Tomás Ó Súilleabháin (Bar), Brian Boydell (cond.)
Mors et Vita, op.50	1961	S.T.B.-soli/Orch: 2222(cbn)/ 4230/perc/SATB chorus	23' 3 movts	Incorporates Timor Mortis, op.35 (1952) Text: William Dunbar, Anon. 16th century	11/1/1963: SFX Hall, Dublin: RÉ Choral Society, RÉSO, Tibor Paul (cond.)
Carmen in Honorem Artis Musicae, op.55	1964	Bar-solo/Orch: 3(pic)121. 2230/timp.perc/pf/SATB chorus	10'	Concert celebrating the bicentenary of the Chair of Music in TCD Text: Donald Wormell	Nov. 1964: TCD: UD Choral Society and Orchestra, Brian Boydell (cond.)
Four Yeats Poems, op.56	1966	S-solo/Orch: 21(ca)22/2200/ perc/hp/str	11' 4 movts	Ded: Gráinne Yeats Adapted from Three Yeats Songs, op.56a and Musician's Song, op.56b	25/2/1969: SFX Hall, Dublin: RTÉSO, Mary Sheridan (S), Brian Boydell (cond.)
A Terrible Beauty is Born, op.59	1965	S.A.B.-soli/Narr/Orch: 2(pic)2(ca) 22(cbn)/4331/ perc/hp/str.SATB chorus	30' 1 movt	Text: Yeats, Ledwidge, MacDonagh, AE, Sigerson, Kettle. Compiled by Tomás Ó Súilleabháin	11/4/1966: Gaiety Theatre, Dublin: RTÉSO, Our Lady's Society, Veronica Dunne (S),

Title	Date	Instrumentation	Duration	Additional Information	First Performance
					Bernadette Greevy (A), William Young (B), Conor Farrington (Narr), Tibor Paul (cond.)
The Carlow Cantata, op.83 (or The Female Friend)	1984	S.T.B.-soli/Orch: 2222/ 4200/hp/timp.perc/str/ SATB chorus or STB-soli/cl.str	35'	Com: Carlow Choral Union Text: Compiled from various authors by Tomás Ó Súilleabháin	10/11/1985: Carlow: Carlow Choral Union, Philip Edmundson (cond.)
Under No Circumstances, op.85 An Historical Entertainment	1987	T.Bar-soli/Orch: 2222/ 2220/timp.perc/pf/org/hpd/ str/Narr/SATB chorus	43'	Com: U.D. Choral Society Text based on Minutes of the Choral Society with original additions by the composer	9/3/1988: TCD: U.D. Choral Society and Orchestra, Peter Kerr, Nigel Williams, Brian Boydell, David Milne (cond.)

SOLO INSTRUMENT AND ORCHESTRA

Title	Date	Instrumentation	Duration	Additional Information	First Performance
Violin Concerto, op.36	1953 rev. 1954	Vn-solo/Orch: 3222/4331/timp.	30'	Ded: Jaroslav Vanacek Com: Jaroslav Vanacek	1/10/1954: Phoenix Hall, Dublin: RÉSO, Jaroslav Vanacek (vn), Milan Horvat (cond.). Revised version: 29/6/1955: Gaiety Theatre, Dublin: RÉSO, Jaroslav Vanacek (vn), Milan Horvat (cond.)
Elegy and Capriccio, op.42	1956	Cl-solo/str orch	14' 2 movts	Ded: Herbert Pöche and the DCO	14/3/1956: Phoenix Hall, Dublin: Chamber Orchestra, Michele Incenzo (cl), Herbert Pöche (cond)
Richard's Riot, op.51	1961	Perc-solo/Orch: 2222/ 4230/str	8' 1 movt	Ded: Richard Callinan	30/11/1961: Ely Hall, Dublin: DOP, Richard Callinan (perc), Brian Boydell (cond.)

CHAMBER MUSIC

Title	Date	Instrumentation	Duration	Additional Information	First Performance
Oboe Quintet, op.11	1940	ob/2vn/va/vc	20' 3 movts	Ded: Betty Kinmonth	10/1/1944: Shelbourne Hotel, Dublin: Carmel Lang (vn), Hazel de Courcey (vn), Máire Larchet (va), Betty Sullivan (vc), Brian Boydell (ob)
String Trio, op.21	1943–1944	vn/va/vc	19' 3 movts	Ded: Ralph Cusack	30/1/1944: Shelbourne Hotel, Dublin: Morris Sinclair (vn), John MacKenzie (va), Betty Sullivan (vc)
The Feather of Death, op.22	1943	Bar-solo/fl/fl/vn/va/vc	12' 3 songs	Song cycle Text: Thurloe Conolly	30/1/1944: Shelbourne Hotel, Dublin: Brian Boydell (Bar), Doris Cleary (fl), Morris Sinclair (vn), John MacKenzie (va), Betty Sullivan (vc)
Sonata for Cello and Piano, op.24	1945	Vc/pf	18' 3 movts	Ded: Betty Sullivan	19/9/1945: National College of Art, Dublin: Betty Sullivan (vc), Charles Lynch (pf)
String Quartet No.1, op.31	1949	2vn/va/vc	20' 3 movts	Rec: DGG 32291/2, Benthien RÉ Chamber Music Prize 1949	17/2/1952: Gresham Hotel, Dublin: Cirulli String Quartet
Divertimento for Three Music Makers, op.38	1954	Ob[fl/vn]/cl[vn/va]/bn [va/vc/cl] Varied choice of instruments	10' 5 movts	Ded: Dublin Chamber Music Group	17/11/1954: RÉ: Les Amis de la Musique
Elegy, op.42a	1955–1956	2vn/vn/cll/pf	7'	Adapted from Elegy and Capriccio, op.42	1957: Jaroslav Vanacek (vn), Kveta Vanacek (vn), Rhoda Coghill (pf)
String Quartet No. 2, op.44	1957	2vn/va/vc	18' 2 movts	Rec: NIRC NIR006, RÉ String Quartet Chandos 9295	14/2/1959: UCC: Benthien String Quartet

Title	Date	Instrumentation	Duration	Additional Information	First Performance
Quintet for Flute, Harp and Strings, op.49	1960 rev. 1966 and 1980	fl/hp/vn/va/vc	17'	Ded: André Prieur and the Prieur Ensemble. Com: Prieur Ensemble	28/6/1960: Shelbourne Hotel, Dublin: Prieur Ensemble
Four Sketches for Two Irish Harps, op.52	1962	2hp(Ir)	10' 4 movts	Ded: Gráinne Yeats and Mercedes Bolger. Com: Gráinne Yeats and Mercedes Bolger. Third sketch is adapted from Dance for an Ancient Ritual, op.39a. Pub: Nos 2 and 3 in Irish Harp Book, Mercier Press, 1975	11/5/1962: Eblana Theatre, Dublin: Gráinne Yeats (Ir.hp),
String Quartet No.3, op.65	1969	2vn/va/vc	20' 1 movt	Ded: RTÉ String Quartet	20/9/1970: National Gallery, Dublin: RTÉ String Quartet
Five Mosaics for Violin and Harp or Piano, op.69	1972	vn/hp[pf]	15' 5 movts	Ded: Geraldine O'Grady Com: Geraldine O'Grady	17/3/1974: RTÉ: Geraldine O'Grady (vn), Havelock Nelson (pf)
Fred's Frolic, op.74a Subtitled: The Adjutant's Ball	1977	Pf (four hands)	10'	Ded: Elizabeth McKim and Winnie Harney Adapted from op.74	1978: TCD: Elizabeth McKim, Winnie Harney
Impetuous Capriccio, op.75a	1978	Vn/pf	3'		
Six Mosaics for Violin and Piano	1978	Vn/pf	20'	op.69 and 75a	
Toccata and Chorale for a State Occasion	1983	2tpt/2hn/2trbn	2'	Com: Arts Council for inauguration of Aosdána	April 1983: House of Lords, Bank of Ireland, Dublin
Ceremonial March	1983	3141/4sax/3413/bass timp.perc	3'		
Five Blows for Brass Quintet	1984	2tpt/hn/trbn/tuba	16'	Com: Joseph Czibi and RTÉ Brass Quintet	14/10/1984: Municipal Gallery, Dublin: RTÉ Brass Quintet

Title	Date	Instrumentation	Duration	Additional Information	First Performance
Confrontations in a Cathedral	1986	Org/hp/perc	10'	Com: Dublin International Organ Festival	23/6/1986: St. Patrick's Cathedral, Dublin Peter Sweeney (org), Denise Kelly (hp)
Adagio and Scherzo for String Quartet, op.89	1991	2vn/va/vc	11'	Written at the request of Professor Hormoz Farhat for the Quartercentenary celebrations of Trinity College, Dublin (1992) Rec: CMC CD 001 May 1995	12/12/1993: TCD: Vanbrugh String Quartet

CHORAL (ACCOMPANIED)

Title	Date	Instrumentation	Duration	Additional Information	First Performance
Timor Mortis, op.35	1952	T-solo/SATB chorus/org[fl/ ob/cl/bn]	10'	Ded: Edgar Deale Text: Anon. 15th century	19/2/1959: Abbey Lecture Hall, Dublin: Clontarf Choral Society, Richard Cooper (T), Eric Hinds (org), Brian Boydell (cond.)
Noël, op.41	1956	2d.rec/2Tr.voices/str orch[org]	3'	Ded: Brook House School Pub: Curwen 1960	1957: Monkstown Parish Church: Pupils of Brook House School
The Small Bell, op.76	1980	SATB chorus/ fl/hp/2vn/va/vc	15' 5 movts	Ded: Tomás Ó Súilleabháin Com: RTÉ	5/5/1981: National Gallery, Dublin: RTÉ Singers, Elizabeth Gaffney (fl), Catríona Yeats (hp), Testore String Quartet
I will hear what God the Lord will speak op.86	1988	SATB/org	5'	Com: Dean of St. Patrick's Cathedral Psalm 85	26/6/1988: St. Patrick's Cathedral Choir, John Dexter (cond.)

CHORAL (UNACCOMPANIED)

Title	Date	Instrumentation	Duration	Additional Information	First Performance
An Easter Carol, op.12	1940	S.T.B/-soli/SATB chorus a cappella	5'	Text: Anon.	22/3/1943: Leinster Hall, Dublin: The Sylphan Singers, Sylvia Fannin (cond.)

Title	Date	Instrumentation	Duration	Additional Information	First Performance
Shatter Me, Music, op.33	1952	SSATB chorus a cappella	2'	Ded: Hans Waldemar Rosen Text: Rilke. Trans: Leishman	7/1/1953: Archbishop Byrne Hall, Dublin
The Owl and the Pussy Cat, op.34	1952	SATB chorus a cappella	3'	Ded: Joseph Groocock Text: Edward Lear	1953: RÉ: RÉ Singers, Hans Waldemar Rosen (cond.)
Two Madrigals, op.54	1964	SSATBB/SATB chorus a cappella	6'	Ded: Dowland Consort Com: WD and HO Wills for Cork International Choral Festival Text: Come Sleep - John Fletcher, I Loved a Lass - George Wither Pub: No.2 Curwen 1964	23/5/1964: Cork International Choral Festival: Dowland Consort, Brian Boydell (cond.)
Three Madrigals, op.60	1967	SATB/SSATB chorus a cappella	9'	Ded: RTÉ Singers Text: O My thoughts Surcease – Philip Sydney, Who shall have my fair lady - Anon. 15th century Adieu, Darling - Anon. 16th century Rec: NIRC NIR007, RTÉ Singers, Hans Waldemar Rosen (cond.)	June 1968: TCD: RTÉ Singers, Hans Waldemar Rosen (cond)
College Graces, op.62	1967	Bar-solo/ SATB chorus a cappella	3' 2 movts	Texts: Trad.	
How, Butler! How, op.67	1971	TTBB chorus a cappella	1.5'	Ded: Larry, the College butler in TCD. Text: 16th century	July 1971: TCD: TCD Choir, Brian Boydell (cond.)
Mouth Music for Ten Voices, op.72	1974	SSSSAATTBB	12' 3 movts	Ded: RTÉ Singers Com: Messrs. Players Wills for the Cork International Choral Festival	27/4/1974: Cork International Choral Festival: RTÉ Singers, Hans Waldemar Rosen (cond.)
Mouth Music for Eight Voices, op.72a	1974	SSAATTBB	12' 3 movts	Ded: Ortetto Vocale Italiano Adapted from op.72	

Title	Date	Instrumentation	Duration	Additional Information	First Performance
Three Geological Glees, op.77	1981	SATB chorus a cappella	9' 3 movts	Ded: Geology Department, TCD Text: Brian Boydell	12/1/1982: Dublin Festival of 20th century Music: Eric Sweeney Singers, Eric Sweeney (cond.)
Monks and Raisins, op.79	1983	ATBarB	4'		
Fuga Con Capo e Coda Senza Corpo	1993	SATB chorus a cappella	2'		
SOLO VOICE (ACCOMPANIED)					
'Wild Geese', op.1	1935	Low voice/pf	2'	Ded: K.A. Stubbs, Director of Music at Rugby School Text: P.H.B. Lyon	1937: Cambridge Music Club: Brian Boydell (Bar)
Rushlights, op.3	1935	Low voice/pf	2'	Ded: W.R. Fearon Text: Anon. Extract from TCD magazine	1937: Cambridge Music Club: Brian Boydell (Bar)
Cathleen, the Daughter of Hoolihan, op.4	1936	Low voice/pf	3'	Ded: Charles Acton Text: W.B.Yeats	
She Weeps Over Rahoon, op.5	1936	Low voice/pf	2'	Text: James Joyce	
Watching the Needleboats at San Sabba	1936 rev. 1937	Low voice/pf	2'	Maurice Pettit Text: James Joyce	
Cradle Song, op.10 no.3	1937 rev. 1943	S/pf	2'	Ded: John Berryman Text: John Berryman	
The Witch, op.6	1938	Low voice/pf	1'	Text: W.B. Yeats	
A Child's Grace, op.10 no.1	1938 rev. 1943	S/pf	2'	Ded: P.B. Kinmonth Text: Robert Herrick	
Aurelia, op.7	1939	Low voice/pf	2'	Ded: P.B. Kinmonth Text: Robert Nichols	

Title	Date	Instrumentation	Duration	Additional Information	First Performance
The Bargain, op.10 no.2	1940 rev. 1943	S/pf	1'	Ded: Marie Werner Text: Sir Philip Sydney	
Three Songs for Soprano and String Quartet, op.10	1943	S/2vn/va/vc	6'	Ded: P.B. Kinmonth, Marie Werner, John Berryman Texts: Robert Herrick, Sir Philip Sydney, John Berryman Versions of: A Child's Grace (1938), The Bargain (1940), Cradle Song (1937)	30/1/1944: Shelbourne Hotel, Dublin: Mary Jones (S), Carmel Lang (vn), Hazel de Courcy (vn), Máira Larchet (va), Betty Sullivan (vc)
Alone, op.15	1941	Low voice/pf	2'	Ded: G.B. Keys Text: James Joyce	
The Lamenting, op.19	1942	Bar-solo/str orch [pf]	2'	Text: Nigel Heseltine	
Sleep Now, op.23	1944	S/ob[vn]/str orch	3'	Text: James Joyce	1/3/1945: Metropolitan Hall, Dublin: DOP; Mary Jones (S), Brian Boydell (cond.)
Five Joyce Songs, op.28	1946	Bar/pf	15'	Ded: Frederick Fuller Text: James Joyce Strings in the Earth and Air, Gentle Lady, It was out by Donnycarney, Rain has fallen all the Day, I hear an army See also op.28a	28/10/1946: Gresham Hotel, Dublin: Brian Boydell (Bar), Joseph Groocock (pf)
Because Your Voice was at my Side, op.25	1948	High voice/pf [ob-d'a/vn/va/vc]	2'	Ded: Mary Boydell Text: James Joyce	
Three Yeats Songs, op.56a	1965	S/Ir hp	9'	Ded: Gráinne Yeats Text: W.B. Yeats	24/3/1966: Abbey Lecture Hall, Dublin: Gráinne Yeats [S/Ir hp]
Musician's Song, op.56b	1965	S/Ir hp	2'	Ded: Gráinne Yeats Com: RTÉ, Song for the play Deirdre	

Title	Date	Instrumentation	Duration	Additional Information	First Performance
Two Yeats Songs	1966	High voice/pf		Musician's Song and Drinking Song	
In Memoriam Thomas Mc Donagh, op.59a	1966	A/pf	3'	Text: Francis Ledwidge Adapted from op.59	31/3/1968: Hibernian Hotel, Dublin: Bernardette Greevy (A), Jeannie Reddin (pf)

SOLO INSTRUMENTAL

Title	Date	Instrumentation	Duration	Additional Information	First Performance
Nine Variations on the Snowy Breasted Pearl, op.2	1935	pf	12'		
Berceuse for a Young Pianist, op.20	1943	pf	2'	Ded: Mary Hoban	
Suite: Naughty Children, op.27	1945	pf	8' 3 movts	Com: Estelle Wine Pub: No. 2, Ricordi, 1959 Go to Sleep, op.27a only, under the title The Sleeping Leprechaun	
Sleeping Leprechaun, op.27a	1945	pf		Go To Sleep, op.27a under the title The Sleeping Leprechaun Pub: Ricordi 1959	
Shielmartin, op.45	1958	pf	3'		
Dance for an Ancient Ritual, op.39a	1959	pf	2'	Pub: Ricordi, 1959 Rec: NIRC 001, Charles Lynch (pf) Adapted from Megalithic Ritual Dances, op.39 (1956)	
Capriccio, op.48	1959	pf	3'	Rec: NIRC 001, Charles Lynch (pf)	7/11/1963: TCD: Havelock Nelson (pf)
Sarabande, op.53	1963	pf	2'	Ded: Joseph Groocock Pub: Ricordi (1964)	7/11/1963: TCD: Havelock Nelson (pf)
A Pack of Fancies for a Travelling Harper, op.66	1970	hp	16' 5 movts	Ded: Una O'Donovan Com: Dublin Festival of 20th century Music	13/1/1971: Dublin Festival of 20th century Music Una O'Donovan (hp)

Title	Date	Instrumentation	Duration	Additional Information	First Performance
Three Pieces for Guitar, op.70	1973	gui	10'	Ded: Siegfried Behrend	9/1/1974: Dublin Festival of 20th century Music
			3 movts	Com: Dublin Festival of 20th century Music	Siegfried Behrend (gui)
An Album of Pieces for the Irish Harp, op.88	1989	Ir hp	20'	Com:Therese Lawlor	23/4/1990: National Concert Hall, Dublin: Therese Lawlor (hp)
The Maiden and the Seven Devils, op.90	1991–1992	pf	5'	Com:GPA Dublin International Piano Competition Pub: CMC in Piano Album 1993	22/5/1994: National Concert Hall, Dublin: Competitors in competition
INCIDENTAL MUSIC					
The House of Cards, op.18	1942	2pf		Incidental music to the play by Frank Carney	1942: Olympia Theatre, Dublin: Brian Boydell (pf), E.W. Boucher (pf)
The Wooing of Etain, op.37	1954	Orch: 2(pic)2(ca)22/4331/timp. perc/cel.hp/str		Incidental music to the play by Padraig Fallon	28/10/1956: RÉ
Yeats Country, op.57	1965	Fl/ob/cl/bn/perc/hp		Com: Patrick Carey Incidental music for the film by Patrick Carey	2/4/1965: Astor Cinema, Dublin
Ireland, op.58	1965	Orch: 2222/4321/perc/str		Com: Vincent Corcoran Incidental music for the film by Vincent Corcoran	17/04/67
Mists of Time, op.61	1967	Orch: Ca/cbn/4hn/perc/str		Com: Patrick Carey Incidental music for the film by Patrick Carey	
Errigal, op.63	1968	Orch: Fl/cbsn/4hn/perc/hp/pf[cel. hpd]/vn/va/vc/tape		Com: Patrick Carey Incidental music for the film by Patrick Carey	July 1968: Academy Cinema

Title	Date	Instrumentation	Duration	Additional Information	First Performance
King Herod Explains, op.68	1971	Mz.S/hp/gong	2' 3 movts	Com: Dublin Gate Theatre Incidental music to the play by Conor Cruise O'Brien	1971: Gate Theatre, Dublin
Miss Julie Music, op.71	1974	S/rebec/gui/perc	3 movts	Com: Gate Theatre, Dublin Incidental music to the play by Strindberg	13/3/1975: Gate Theatre, Dublin
BAND MUSIC					
Viking Lip – Music, op.91	1996	2tpt/2cornet/2hn/3trbn/ euphonium tuba/2perc	9'	Com: Music Network for Royal Danish Brass	5/11/1996: Drogheda Arts Centre: Royal Danish Brass
Fred's Frolic, op.74 (Band) Subtitled: The Adjutant's Ball	1977	(pic)2141/a.sax/t.sax/ bar.sax/3432/2bass timp/ 2perc	10'	Ded: Fred O'Callaghan and the Army No.1 Band. Com: Fred O'Callaghan and the Army No.1 Band	1978: TCD: Army No.1 Band, Fred O'Callaghan (cond.)
ARRANGEMENTS					
The National Anthem of Ireland	1961	Orch		Arr. for RTÉ	
The Robin in Winter	1963	Solo song		Text: English trad.	

Writings by Brian Boydell

Compiled by AXEL KLEIN

CULTURAL CRITICISM

'Music in Ireland', *The Bell*, 14, 1 (1947), pp.16–20, with replies by Aloys Fleischmann (ibid., pp.20–4) and Michael Bowles (ibid., pp.24–5).

'Culture and Chauvinism', *Envoy*, 2 (May 1950), pp.75–9.

'The Future of Music in Ireland', *The Bell*, 16, 4 (1951), pp.1–9, with replies by Aloys Fleischmann (Vol. 16, No. 5, pp.5–10), P.J. Malone (ibid., pp.10–13), Joseph O'Neill (ibid., pp.13–18).

'Orchestral and Chamber Music in Dublin', in Aloys Fleischmann (ed.), *Music in Ireland: A Symposium* (Cork: Cork University Press and Oxford Blackwell, 1952), pp.222–31.

'Half a Century of Music in Dublin', *Dublin Historical Record*, 37, 3, 4 (1984), pp.117–21.

'RTÉ's Commitment to Contemporary Irish Music', *New Music News* (January 1991), p.3.

'New Harmonic Horizons', *The Irish Times*, 4 March 1992.

'The Roaring Forties and Thereabouts' (unpublished autobiography of 1993–94).

HISTORICAL MUSICOLOGY

'John Field', *Ireland of the Welcomes*, 18, 4 (1969), pp.18–21.

'Venues for Music in 18th-century Dublin', *Dublin Historical Record*, 29, 1 (1975), pp.28–34.

'The Dublin Musical Scene 1749–50 and its Background', *Proceedings of the Royal Musical Association*, 105 (1978–79), pp.77–89.

Four Centuries of Music in Ireland, Edited (London: BBC, 1979) including 'Introduction', pp.10–12, and 'Music in Eighteenth-Century Dublin', pp.28–38.

Articles on: Richard Broadway, Edward Bunting, Philip Cogan, James Colgan, Davis [family], Henry Delamain, Dublin, Matthew Dubourg, Aloys Fleischmann, Thomas Augustine Geary, Hollister [family], Francis Ireland, Walker Jackson, Samuel Lee, William Manwaring, John Ogilby, Kane O'Hara, Burk Thumoth, William Viner, Joseph Cooper Walker, Wexford, Woffington [family], and Richard Woodward in Stanley Sadie (ed.), *The New Grove Dictionary of Music and Musicians* (London: Macmillan, 1980).

Articles on: John Egan, Hollister [family], Henry William Rother, Ferdinand Weber, and Woffington [family] in: Stanley Sadie (ed.), *The New Grove Dictionary of Musical Instruments* (London: Macmillan, 1984).

'Georgian Lollipops, or, The Lighter Side of Classical Music', in Hugh Shields (ed.), *Popular Music in Eighteenth-Century Dublin* (Dublin: Folk Music Society of Ireland, 1985), pp.5–11.

'Music before 1700', in T.W. Moody and W.E. Vaughan (eds), *A New History of Ireland*, Vol. IV (Oxford: Oxford University Press, 1986), pp.542–67.

'Music 1700–1850', ibid., Vol. 8, pp.568–628.

'Music', in Ian Campbell Ross (ed.), *Publick Virtue, Publick Love: The*

Early Years of the Dublin Lying-in Hospital (Dublin: O'Brien Press, 1986), pp.96–125.

A Dublin Musical Calendar 1700–1760 (Dublin: Irish Academic Press, 1988).

'The Virgin Mary in Music', *Milltown Studies*, 22 (Autumn 1988), pp.87–9.

'Thomas Bateson and the Earliest Degrees in Music awarded by the University of Dublin', *Hermathena*, 146 (Summer 1989), pp.53–60.

'Music at the Rotunda Gardens 1771–91', in Gerard Gillen and Harry White (eds.), *Musicology in Ireland (Irish Musical Studies 1)* (Dublin: Irish Academic Press, 1990), pp.99–116.

'Mr. Pockrich and the Musical Glasses', *Dublin Historical Record*, 44, 2 (1991), pp.25–33.

Articles on: Philip Cogan, Dublin, T.J. Walsh in: Stanley Sadie (ed.), *The New Grove Dictionary of Opera* (London: Macmillan, 1992).

Rotunda Music in Eighteenth-Century Dublin (Dublin: Irish Academic Press, 1992).

'Handel's Visit to Dublin', *Ireland of the Welcomes*, 41, 2 (1992), pp.34–9.

'Jonathan Swift and the Dublin Musical Scene', *Dublin Historical Record*, 47, 2 (1994), pp.132–8.

'Organs Associated with Handel's Visit to Dublin', *Journal of the British Institute of Organ Studies*, 119 (1995), pp.54–74.

Articles on: Richard Broadway, Edward Bunting, Philip Cogan, James Colgan, Davis [family], Henry Delamain, Dublin, Matthew Dubourg, Thomas Augustine Geary, Hollister [family], Francis Ireland, Samuel Lee, William Manwaring, John Ogilby, Kane O'Hara, Burk Thumoth, William Viner, Woffington [family],

Margaret Woffington, and Richard Woodward in Stanley Sadie (ed.), *The New Grove Dictionary of Music and Musicians*, 2nd edition (London: Macmillan, 2001).

Articles on: Matthew Dubourg, Thomas Augustine Geary, Francis Ireland, Kane O'Hara, John O'Keeffe, Richard Pockrich, and William Viner in Ludwig Finscher (ed.), *Die Musik in Geschichte und Gegenwart*, rev. edn, Biographical Section (Kassel: Metzler, 1999–2007).

Bibliography

Compiled by AXEL KLEIN

Acton, Charles. 'Music Makers Portrait Gallery', *Irish Times*, 2 July 1960.

——, 'Interview with Brian Boydell', *Éire-Ireland*, 5, 4 (1970), pp.97–111.

——, 'Brian Patrick Boydell', *Irish Arts Review*, 4, 4 (1987), pp.66–7.

Battersby, Eileen. 'Brian's double forte', *Irish Times*, 6 November 1997.

Bodley, Seóirse. 'Boydell, Brian', in Stanley Sadie (ed.), *The New Grove Dictionary of Music and Musicians* (London: Macmillan, 1980), Vol. 3, p.144.

Cox, Gareth. 'Octatonicism in the String Quartets of Brian Boydell', in: Patrick F. Devine and Harry White (eds.), *The Maynooth International Musicological Conference 1995: Selected Proceedings Part One (Irish Musical Studies 4)* (Dublin: Four Courts Press, 1996), pp.263–70.

——, 'Boydell, Brian', in Stanley Sadie (ed.), *The New Grove Dictionary of Music and Musicians*, 2nd edn (London: Macmillan, 2001), Vol. 4, pp.163–4.

Deale, Edgar M. *A Catalogue of Contemporary Irish Composers* (Dublin: Music Association of Ireland, 1968), 1972.

Donoghue, Denis. 'The Future of Irish Music', *Studies*, 44 (Spring 1955), pp.109–14.

Doyle, Niall (ed.). *The Boydell Papers: Essays on Music and Music Policy in Ireland* (Dublin: Music Network, 1997).

Dungan, Michael. 'Everything Except Team Games and Horse-Racing', *New Music News* (February 1997), pp.9–11.

Fallon, Brian. *An Age of Innocence: Irish Culture 1930–1960* (Dublin: Gill & Macmillan, 1998).

Farrell, Hazel. 'The String Quartets of Brian Boydell' (MA thesis, Waterford Institute of Technology, 1996).

Fleischmann, Aloys (ed.). *Music in Ireland: A Symposium* (Cork: Cork University Press and Oxford: Blackwell, 1952).

——, 'Boydell, Brian', in Eric Blom (ed.), [Grove's] *A Dictionary of Music and Musicians*, Supplementary vol. (London: Macmillan, 1961), pp.45–6.

——, 'Brian Boydell', *Hibernia*, 32, 9 (1968).

——, 'Boydell, Brian (Patrick)', in Brian Morton and Pamela Collins (eds.), *Contemporary Composers* (Chicago and London: St James Press, 1992), pp.110–13.

Gillen, Gerard. 'Boydell, Brian', in W.J. McCormack (ed.), *The Blackwell Companion to Modern Irish Culture* (Oxford: Blackwell, 1999), p.78.

Graydon, Philip. 'Modernism in Ireland and its Cultural Context in the Music and Writings of Frederick May, Brian Boydell and Aloys Fleischmann' (MA thesis, National University of Ireland, Maynooth, 1999), also in G. Cox and A. Klein, *Irish Music in the Twentieth Century* (Irish Musical Studies, 7) (Dublin: Four Courts Press, 2003).

Kennedy, Brian P. *Dreams and Responsibilities: The State and the Arts in Independent Ireland* (Dublin: The Arts Council, 1990, 2nd edn 1998).

Klein, Axel. 'Brian Boydell', in Walter-Wolfgang Sparrer and Hans-Werner Heister (eds.), *Komponisten der Gegenwart* (Munich: edition text + kritik, 1992 *ff* [November 1994]).

——, *Die Musik Irlands im 20. Jahrhundert* (Hildesheim: Georg Olms Verlag, 1996).

——, 'Irish Composers and Foreign Education: A Study of Influences', in Patrick F. Devine and Harry White (eds.), *The Maynooth International Musicological Conference 1995: Selected Proceedings Part One (Irish Musical Studies 4)* (Dublin: Four Courts Press, 1996), pp.271–84.

——, 'The Composer in the Academy (2) 1940–1990', in Richard Pine and Charles Acton (eds.), *To Talent Alone: The Royal Irish Academy of Music 1848–1998* (Dublin: Gill and Macmillan, 1998), pp.415–23.

——, 'Boydell, Brian (Patrick)', in Ludwig Finscher (ed.), *Die Musik in Geschichte und Gegenwart*, new edn., Biographical Section, Vol. 3 (Kassel: Bärenreiter and Stuttgart: Metzler, 2000), 600–2.

Lee, David. 'Boydell, Brian', in Friedrich Blume (ed.) *Die Musik in Geschichte und Gegenwart* (MGG), 1st supplement volume, (Kassel: Bärenreiter, 1973), 1031–2

Murphy, Daniel *et al.* (eds.). 'Brian Boydell', *Education and the Arts*, chapter XXII (Dublin: Trinity College, 1987), pp.219–29.

O'Kelly, Eve. 'An On-Going Tradition', *New Music News* (May 1992), pp.7–9, 18.

O'Kelly, Pat. *The National Symphony Orchestra of Ireland 1948–1998: A Selected History* (Dublin: RTÉ, 1998).

Ryan, Joseph J. 'Nationalism and Music in Ireland' (PhD diss., National University of Ireland, 1991).

Discography

Compiled by AXEL KLEIN

In memoriam Mahatma Gandhi, **op. 30** (1948) for orchestra
- National Symphony Orchestra of Ireland, Colman Pearce (cond): Marco Polo 8.223887. CD 1997.

String Quartet No. 1, op. 31 (1949)
- Benthien Streichquartett: Deutsche Grammophon 32291. LP 1955?.
- Academica Quartet: Goasco GXX 002-4. MC 1985.

Violin Concerto, op. 36 (1953–54)
- Maighread McCrann (vn), National Symphony Orchestra of Ireland, Colman Pearce (cond): Marco Polo 8.223887. CD 1997.

Megalithic Ritual Dances, op. 39 (1956) for orchestra
- Radio Éireann Symphony Orchestra, Milan Horvat (cond): Decca (USA) DL 9843. LP 1958.
- National Symphony Orchestra of Ireland, Colman Pearce (cond): Marco Polo 8.223887. CD 1997.

Noël op. 41 (1956) satb, 2rec, org
- TCDCC03 (CD, 2000): Jennifer Kelly (rec), Alison Gillespie (rec), Michael Quinn (org), Trinity College Dublin Chapel Choir, Simon Harden (cond).

String Quartet No. 2, op. 44 (1957)
- Vanbrugh Quartet: Chandos CHAN 9295. CD 1994.

Dance for an Ancient Ritual, op. 39a (1959) for piano

• Charles Lynch: New Irish Recording Co. NIR 001. LP 1971.

Capriccio, op. 48 (1959) for piano
• Charles Lynch: New Irish Recording Co. NIR 001. LP 1971.

Three Yeats Songs, op. 56a (1965) for voice and piano or harp
• Gráinne Yeats (v, hp): Columbia (Japan) JX-32. LP 1972?.

Symphonic Inscapes, **op. 64** (1968) for orchestra
• RTÉ Symphony Orchestra, Albert Rosen (cond): New Irish Recording Co. NIR 011. LP 1975.

A Pack of Fancies for a Travelling Harper op. 66 (1970) hp
• Riverrun RRCD (CD, 2003): Clíona Doris.

Three Pieces, op. 70 (1973) for guitar
• John Feeley: Black Box Music BBM 1002. CD 1998.

Masai Mara, op. 87 (1988) for orchestra
• National Symphony Orchestra of Ireland, Colman Pearce (cond): Marco Polo 8.223887. CD 1997.

Adagio and Scherzo, **op. 89** (1991) for string quartet
• Vanbrugh Quartet: CMC CD01. Promotion-CD 1995.

Viking Lip-Music, op. 91 (1996) for brass band
• Royal Danish Brass: Rondo Grammofon RCD 8358. CD 1997.

Also:
String Quartet No. 2, op. 44 (1957)
• RTÉ String Quartet: NIR 006 LP 1973.
Three Madrigals, **op. 60** (1967), satb., NIR 007 1974.
Both intended for New Irish Recording Co., recorded but never released.

Notes

1. Much of the detailed biographical information on Brian Boydell in this chapter is taken from, or based on, a manuscript autobiography written in 1994, 'The Roaring Forties and Thereabouts'. My sincere thanks go to the composer for letting me use this fascinating account of his experiences until about the mid-1960s. A photocopy of this manuscript is now in the library of the Contemporary Music Centre, Dublin.
2. Boydell in the Network 2-broadcast *All My Enthusiasms*, produced by Anne Makeower, January 1998.
3. Boydell, 'The Roaring Forties', p.4.
4. According to Philip Graydon, Boydell's paternal grandmother and aunt did encourage the boy to pursue his musical interests, the former having been an early visitor to Bayreuth and the latter a 'fairly good amateur pianist', Philip Graydon, 'Modernism in Ireland and its Cultural Context in the Music and Writings of Frederick May, Brian Boydell and Aloys Fleischmann' (MA thesis, National University of Ireland, Maynooth, 1999), p.77. In contrast to his father, Brian Boydell was able to give the education of his own children a different direction, described by his son Barra as a most 'liberal and open upbringing', rare for its time. 'He was not in any way authoritarian as a father: we were very much brought up to think out for ourselves the consequences of our actions, rather than having behaviour imposed from above' (communicated in an e-mail dated 3 March 2000).
5. Boydell, *The Roaring Forties*, p.6.
6. Ibid., p.8.
7. Ibid., p.10.
8. Ibid., p.12.
9. Ibid., p.15a.
10. Ibid., p.60.
11. Ibid.
12. Charles Acton, 'Brian Patrick Boydell', *Irish Arts Review* 4, 4 (1987), pp.66–7. The following quotation is from p.67.
13. Boydell, 'The Roaring Forties', pp.47–8.
14. Quoted from a copy of the original letter from Brian Boydell to 41 composers, dated 9 November 1949.
15. In 1976 the Composers' Group merged with the Association of Young Irish Composers (est. 1972) to form the Association of Irish Composers (AIC), which since 1985 constitutes the Irish membership of the ISCM.
16. Edgar M. Deale, *A Catalogue of Contemporary Irish Composers* (Dublin: MAI, 1968, 1972).
17. Boydell, 'The Roaring Forties', p.72.

18. See Pat O'Kelly, *The National Symphony Orchestra of Ireland 1948–1998* (Dublin: RTÉ 1998). By the end of the 1930s the station orchestra had already numbered almost thirty musicians and was often supplemented from various sources for larger works. From 1941 to 1947 the orchestra had appeared regularly in public, creating for the first time a large audience for symphonic music. What took place in 1948 was an enlargement and a renaming of the orchestra, which happened again in 1990 as the NSOI.
19. Boydell, 'The Roaring Forties', p.74.
20. Side B featured Seóirse Bodley's *Music for Strings* and three of the five movements of Frederick May's *Suite of Irish Airs* (see Discography).
21. Boydell, 'The Roaring Forties', p.78.
22. Denis Donoghue, 'The Future of Irish Music', *Studies*, 44 (Spring 1955), p.110.
23. Ibid.
24. Ibid.
25. Brian Boydell, 'Music in Ireland', *The Bell*, 14 (April 1947), pp.16–17.
26. Ibid., p.17.
27. Brian Boydell, 'Culture and Chauvinism', *Envoy*, 2 (May 1950), p.75.
28. Ibid., p.77.
29. This topic has been comprehensively discussed by Philip Graydon ('Modernism in Ireland'), p.4.
30. Brian Boydell, 'The Future of Music in Ireland', *The Bell*, 16 (January 1951).
31. Ibid., p.21.
32. Ibid.
33. Ibid., p.22.
34. Walter Beckett (1914–96), Thomas C. Kelly (1917–85), Redmond Friel (1907–79) and Éamonn Ó Gallchobháir (1906–82) were composers with only few original compositions to their credit. Their music was based on Irish traditional melody, often skilful and attractive in its own right, albeit completely removed from the developments of contemporary classical music – which is why they disqualified themselves from serious critical attention. As a phenomenon peculiar to Ireland, their music would, however, deserve more attention today as 'light' classical music appears to have established new audiences.
35. Charles Acton, 'Music Makers Portrait Gallery', *Irish Times*, 2 July 1960, p.8. It should be added at this point that the two composers for whom Acton saw the greatest potential were Ó Riada and Bodley.
36. Michael Dungan, 'Everything Except Team Games and Horse Racing', *New Music News* (February 1997), p.10. The following quote is from the same source.
37. *Timor Mortis* was later incorporated into the cantata *Mors et vita*, op. 50 (1961).
38. Charles Acton, 'Interview with Brian Boydell', *Éire-Ireland*, 4 (1970), pp.108–9.
39. Charles Acton, 'R.T.É.S.O.'s fine playing for Rosen', *Irish Times*, 27 January 1969.
40. Dungan, 'Everything Except team Games', p.10.
41. Acton, 'Interview with Brian Boydell.
42. Father Donal O'Sullivan SJ was Director of the Arts Council from 1960 to 1973.

43. Brian P. Kennedy, *Dreams and Responsibilities: The State and the Arts in Independent Ireland* (Dublin: The Arts Council, undated [1990], 2nd edn 1998), p.138.
44. Boydell, 'The Roaring Forties', p.88.
45. Ibid., p.89.
46. Ibid., p.86.
47. Charles Acton's review of that concert can be found in Gareth Cox (ed.), *Acton's Music: Reviews of Dublin's Musical Life 1955–1985* (Bray, Co. Wicklow: Kilbride Books, 1996), pp.67–9.
48. Both quotes from Boydell, 'The Roaring Forties', p. 87.
49. Ibid., p.90.
50. Ibid., p.92. Michael Dungan in his 1997 article on Boydell relates that their time for an interview was limited because the 'Dowland Consort … is coming round for one of its quarterly evenings of dining, conviviality and Renaissance madrigals'. He motions to a stack of scores resting on the piano. 'Ensemble vocal music to me is just the tops. And you see', he adds with a funny mixture of mischief and pride, 'I sit at the end of the table and direct. It's the greatest pleasure I have.' Dungan, 'Everything Except Team Games', p.9.
51. In Eve O'Kelly, 'An On-going Tradition', *New Music News* (May 1992), p.7.
52. In Acton, 'Interview with Brian Boydell', p.99. The next quotation is from the same page.

NOTES TO CHAPTER 2

1. Gareth Cox, 'Octatonicism in the String Quartets of Brian Boydell', in Patrick F. Devine and Harry White (eds.), *The Maynooth International Musicological Conference 1995: Selected Proceedings Part One (Irish Musical Studies 4)*, (Dublin: Four Courts Press, 1996), p.270.
2. Boydell in interview with Charles Acton, *Éire-Ireland*, 5, 4 (1970), p.104.
3. Boydell in the *Irish Times*, 4 March 1992. In another list of influences in Brian Morton and Pamela Collins (eds.), *Contemporary Composers* (Chicago and London: St James Press, 1992), p.112, he also mentions Bloch.
4. Hazel Farrell, 'The String Quartets of Brian Boydell' (MA thesis, NCEA [Waterford Institute of Technology], 1996), p.17.
5. Charles Acton, *Irish Times*, 20 November 1969.
6. Acton, *Éire-Ireland*, 5, 4 (1970), p.104.
7. Morton and Collin, *Contemporary Composers*, p.112.
8. Brian Boydell in interview with Eileen Battersby, *Irish Times*, 6 November 1997.
9. Morton and Collins, *Contemporary Composers*, p.112.
10. Contemporary Music Centre, Ireland Composer Catalogue, 7th edn, 1999.
11. Pieter van den Toorn, *Stravinsky and 'The Rite of Spring': The Beginnings of a Musical Language* (Oxford: Oxford University Press, 1987) and Allen Forte, *The Atonal Music of Anton Webern* (New Haven: Yale University Press, 1998) and *The Structure of Atonal Music* (New Haven: Yale University Press, 1973).
12. Eve O'Kelly, 'An On-going Tradition', *New Music News* (May 1992), p.8.
13. Robin Hartwell, 'Postmodernism and Art Music', in Simon Miller (ed.), *Music*

and Society: The Last Post (Manchester: Manchester University Press, 1993), p.28.

14. RTÉ, 28 June 1989. Manuscript text in the Contemporary Music Centre, Ireland in Dublin.

15. Brian Boydell, Lecture Notes, undated.

16. Joel Lester, *Analytical Approaches to Twentieth-Century Music* (New York: Norton, 1989, p.167.

17. After Allen Forte 1998, *Atonal Music of Anton Webern*, p.11. Model A (ascending 1–2–1) begins with a semitone, Model B (descending 2–1–2) with a tone.

18. Cox, 'Octatonicism in the String Quartets of Brian Boydell', p.268.

19. Cited in Cox, ibid., p.268

20. Joseph Ryan, 'Nationalism and Music in Ireland' (PhD, National University of Ireland, 1991), p.432f.

21. Programme Booklet in the Contemporary Music Centre, Dublin.

22. Boydell, RTÉ Broadcast, 28 June 1989.

23. O'Kelly, *New Music News* (May 1992), p.8.

24. Acton, *Éire-Ireland*, 5, 4 (1970), p.106.

25. Boydell, Programme Note for the 20th Century Music 3rd Dublin Festival 1971, p.20.

26. Allen Forte, 'Debussy and the Octatonic', *Music Analysis*, 10: 1–2 (1991), p.127.

27. Morton and Collins, *Contemporary Composers*, p.112.

28. Acton, *Éire-Ireland*, 5, 4 (1970), p.105. See also Axel Klein, *Die Musik Irlands im 20. Jahrhundert* (Hildesheim: Georg Olms Verlag, 1996), pp.229–330.

29. Undated Lecture Notes kindly provided by the composer.

30. Marie Donnelly (ed.) (Dublin: Irish Hospice Foundation, 1999).

31. Boydell mentioned in an RTÉ broadcast, 28 June 1989, that this final theme was inspired by the *Rejouissance* of Bach's Orchestral Suite No. 4.

32. Morton and Collins, *Contemporary Composers*, p.113.

33. Philip Graydon, 'Modernism in Ireland and its Cultural Context in the Music and Writings of Frederick May, Brian Boydell and Aloys Fleischmann' (MA thesis, National University of Ireland, Maynooth, 1999), p.128.

34. Acton, *Éire-Ireland*, p.105.

35. Graydon, 'Modernism in Ireland', p.104.

36. O'Kelly, *New Music News* (May 1992), p.8.

37. Battersby, *Irish Times*, 6 November 1997, p.8.

NOTES TO CHAPTER 3

1. The phrase is from Joseph Cooper Walker, *Historical Memoirs of the Irish Bards* (Dublin 1786; facsimile reprint New York: Garland, 1971), p.158.

2. See Harry White, 'The Preservation of Music and Irish Cultural History', *International Review of the Aesthetics and Sociology of Music*, 27, 2 (1996), pp.123–38. For a discussion of this debate, see Axel Klein, *Die Musik Irlands im 20. Jahrhundert* (Hildesheim: Georg Olms Verlag, 1996), pp.55–63 and Harry White, *The Keeper's Recital: Music and Cultural History in Ireland, 1770–1970* (Cork: Cork University Press, 1998), pp.129–35.

3. Brian Boydell, 'The Future of Music in Ireland', *The Bell*, 16, 4 (1951), pp.21–9.

4. Brian Boydell, *Rotunda Music in Eighteenth-Century Dublin* (Dublin: Irish Academic Press, 1992), p.11.

5. Roy Foster, *Modern Ireland, 1600–1972* (London: Allen Lane, 1988), p.194.

6. Boydell, *The Bell*, 16, 4 (1951), p.21.

7. For full citations of these publications, see the list of writings by Brian Boydell in Appendix II.

8. Brian Boydell, 'Music, 1700–1850', in T.W. Moody and W.E. Vaughan (eds.), *A New History of Ireland*, Vol. 8 (Oxford: Oxford University Press, 1986), p.568.

9. Boydell, ibid., p.606.

10. I discuss these comments below.

11. I make this point literally with regard to the information provided by Boydell in this book. Nevertheless, these extremes of musical taste (within the art music tradition) are also representative of conflicting ideologies of musical culture within the Ascendancy itself. For a discussion of this matter, see Frank Ll. Harrison, 'Music, Poetry and Polity in the Age of Swift', *Eighteenth-Century Ireland*, 1 (1986), pp.37–64, also White, *The Keeper's Recital*, p.13ff.

12. This is not to suggest that Haydn's music was as frequently performed in the late eighteenth century as was Handel's at mid-century. See Appendix VI in Boydell, *Rotunda Music in Eighteen-Century Dublin*, 'Analysis of music performed, 1771–91', pp.161–70. Nevertheless, as Boydell shows, the music performed at the Dublin concerts closely compares with the corresponding London repertory.

13. Leo Treitler, 'What Kind of Story is History', chapter in Treitler, *Music and the Historical Imagination* (Cambridge, MA: Harvard University Press, 1989), p.173.

14. See, for example, Carl Dahlhaus, *Foundations of Music History* (Cambridge: Cambridge University Press, 1983); Joseph Kerman, 'A Few Canonic Variations', in Robert van Halberg (ed.), *Canons* (Special issue of *Critical Inquiry*, 10 [1983], pp.107–26) and Lydia Goehr, *The Imaginary Museum of Musical Works* (Oxford: Clarendon Press, 1992).

15. Goehr, *The Imaginary Museum of Musical Works*, p.8.

16. The classic instance of this condemnation is J.A. Scheibe's vehement criticism of Bach's manner of composition published in *Der Critische Musikus*, 14 May 1737.

17. See White, *The Keeper's Recital*, p.33. For further discussion of Handel's visit to Dublin, see Donald Burrows, 'Handel's Dublin Performances', in Patrick F. Devine and Harry White (eds.), *The Maynooth International Musicological Conference 1995: Selected Proceedings Part One (Irish Musical Studies 4)* (Dublin: Four Courts Press, 1996), pp.46–70.

18. See the writings of Lawrence Whyte, Oliver Goldsmith and Joseph Cooper Walker discussed in White, *The Keeper's Recital*, p.15 ff.

19. Foster, *Modern Ireland, 1600–1972*, p.185.

20. Walker, *Historical Memoirs of the Irish Bards*, pp.158–61.

21. See Seamus Deane, 'The Literary Myths of the Revival', *Celtic Revivals* (London: Faber and Faber, 1985), pp.128–38.

NOTES TO CHAPTER 4

1. David Sylvester, *The Brutality of Fact: Interviews with Francis Bacon*, 3rd edn (London: Thames and Hudson, 1987), preface.
2. Albert Ketèlbey (1875–1959), British composer of 'In a monastery garden'.
3. British organist and conductor (1897–1961), Director of the choir of King's College, Cambridge.
4. The noted concert pianist Solomon Cutner (1902–88).
5. Patrick Hadley (1899–1973), British composer, later Professor at Cambridge.
6. Léon Goossens (1897–1988), British oboe player.
7. Herbert Howells (1892–1983), British composer, noted for his choral music.
8. Drei kleine Stücke für Violoncello und Klavier, op.11 (1914).
9. Irish pianist (1906–84).
10. John Larchet (1884–1967), Irish composer and teacher.
11. Irish conductor and accompanist (1917–96).
12. Brian Boydell held the Chair in Music from 1962 until his retirement in 1982.
13. Jean Martinon (1910–76), French composer and conductor.
14. Arnold Bax (1883–1953), British composer with strong Irish connections.
15. Alan Rawsthorne (1905–71), British composer.
16. Alois Hába (1893–1973), Czech composer.
17. Klaviersonate, op. 1 (1907–08).
18. First performed complete in 1935.
19. For baritone, chorus and orchestra, first performed in 1931.
20. For reciter and small ensemble, first performed publicly in 1923. Somewhat fancifully regarded as an English *Pierrot Lunaire* (Schoenberg's 1912 cycle).
21. Vier Lieder, op. 2 (1910).
22. Alexander Vasilievich Mosolov (1900–73), Russian composer.
23. Irish composer (1910–92), Professor of Music at University College, Cork.
24. Frederick May (1911–85), Irish composer.
25. Eamonn Ó Gallchobháir (1906–82), Irish composer.
26. T.C. Kelly (1917–85), Irish composer.
27. Irish composer (1907–79).
28. Irish composer (b. 1933).
29. The precursor of the Irish Music Rights Organisation.
30. Charles Acton, 'Interview with Brian Boydell', *Éire Ireland*, 5, 4 (1970), pp.97–111.
31. Charles Kitson (1874–1944), Professor of Music in Trinity College Dublin (1920–35).
32. Joseph Groocock was part-time Lecturer in the School of Music for many years.

Notes on Contributors

GARETH COX graduated from Trinity College Dublin and the University of Freiburg and is Senior Lecturer and Head of the Department of Music at Mary Immaculate College, University of Limerick. His books include *Anton Weberns Studienzeit* (Frankfurt, 1991) and *Irish Music in the Twentieth Century* (Dublin, 2003) edited with Axel Klein. He is a contributor to *The New Grove* and *Die Musik in Geschichte und Gegenwart*.

HAZEL FARRELL wrote an MA on the String Quartets of Brian Boydell in 1996 at Waterford Institute of Technology (where she has taught since 1993) and in 2002 completed a Ph.D. on pitch structure and pitch selection in post-war Irish composition at Mary Immaculate College, University of Limerick.

AXEL KLEIN studied at the universities of Hildesheim and Trinity College Dublin taking his doctorate with the first major study on twentieth-century Irish music, *Die Musik Irlands im 20. Jahrhundert* (Hildesheim, 1996). He has published *Irish Classical Recordings: A Discography of Irish Art Music* (Westport CT, 2001), edited *Irish Music in the Twentieth Century* with Gareth Cox (Dublin, 2003), and has contributed to *The New Grove* and *Die Musik in Geschichte und Gegenwart*.

MICHAEL TAYLOR is Lecturer in Music in Trinity College Dublin. His research interests focus on musical analysis, and on twentieth-century and contemporary music. His most recent publications include the Inventory of the Harrison Birtwistle Collection in the Paul Sacher Stiftung (Basel) and a contribution to the symposium 'Musik Theater Heute'.

HARRY WHITE is Professor of Music at University College Dublin and joint general editor of *Irish Musical Studies*. His books include *The Keeper's Recital: Music and Cultural History in Ireland, 1770–1970* (1998), *Musical Constructions of Nationalism* (2001) edited with Michael Murphy; and *The History of a Baroque Oratorio* (forthcoming in 2003). In May 2003 he was appointed first President of the Society for Musicology in Ireland.

Index